Arizona Ranch Houses

Arizona Ranch Houses

Southern Territorial Styles, 1867–1900

Janet Ann Stewart

Edited by
John Bret Harte

Photographs by
Louis Bencze

University of Arizona Press
and
Arizona Historical Society
Tucson

Copyright © 1974, The Arizona Historical Society

Second Printing 1987
The University of Arizona Press
and Arizona Historical Society
Manufactured in the U.S.A.

Library of Congress Cataloging-in-Publication Data

Stewart, Janet Ann, 1925-
   Arizona ranch houses.

   Reprint. Originally published: Tucson : Arizona
Historical Society, 1974. Originally published in series:
Historical monograph; no. 2.
   Bibliography: p.
   1. Ranch houses—Arizona—History—19th century.
2. Vernacular architecture—Arizona. 3. Regionalism
in architecture—Arizona. I. Bret Harte, John.
II. Title.
[NA7235.A6S83   1987]   728.3 ′7′09791   87-14553

ISBN 0-8165-1045-8 (alk. paper)

British Library Cataloguing in Publication data are available.

Contents

Birth of a Style

The elegant frame-and-adobe Fitch house, about 1885. It bespoke a greater regard for style than for protection against summer temperatures. Tucson's indigenous architecture persists next door.

FRONTIER REGIONAL ARCHITECTURE represented an adaptation by builders of traditional forms to the needs of place and time, as well as an expression of the possibilities inherent in available materials. In southern Arizona a strong architectural heritage existed, ready to greet the influx of Anglo-Americans who entered the region after the Civil War. The dominant forms of this tradition originated in Spain, perhaps going back ultimately, through the Arabs, to Oriental structures which functioned in much the same fashion in environments not too different from those of northern Mexico and southern Arizona.[1] Characteristics of style and building methods employed in Andalusia and neighboring areas were easily transported to regions of New Spain similar in terrain and climate. These importations included massive mudbrick wall and beam construction and the urban courtyard design, as well as the looser derivative form of this design, the country *hacienda* house.[2]

The mudbrick wall and beam system was simple and straightforward, geometric and undetailed. Buildings were hollow cubes with unsophisticated profiles and flat surfaces. To this plain, functional style Spanish and Mexican builders added turned wooden spindles and wrought-iron grill work, reflecting prosperity in this elegance of ornamentation. Such refinements reached a high development in the Sonoran cities of Alamos and Hermosillo but seldom extended farther north onto the frontier. Instead, the Spanish-Mexican construction that most strongly influenced Anglo-American builders developed in less sophisticated settlements, where land and the resources at hand determined the type of structures which arose. Clay and mud became the principal building materials, the length of available wooden roof beams determined room scale, and climate and the needs of defense controlled the size and type of wall openings.[3] Such considerations called for simple, functional architectural forms.

Sometimes a still more primitive structure preceded the true ranch house — a one-room hut of the simplest kind. Alan Gowans is no doubt referring to such temporary buildings (to which he applies the term *jacal*) when he observes that "moving on to new frontier places meant moving back in time to earlier and more primitive worlds. It meant building not 'architecture' but . . . something more like birds piecing a nest together." The permanent adobe houses were more sophisticated than that, plain as they were. They epitomized a folk or vernacular idiom, pre-industrial, additive and open ended, which contributed much to construction in Arizona's territorial years.[4]

The Spanish-Mexican urban house and antecedents dated back to the atrium house of the Roman Republic and Empire. From this structure there evolved in Spain a courtyard residence which made private living possible in an urban situation.[5] The original site for this type of house was the city or village square with the church, the focus of community life, on one side and grid-plan streets radiating from it. Introduced into the municipal centers of Mexico, these courtyard houses, edging city blocks, developed an urban texture of land utilization both rational and aesthetically satisfying. They presented a massive, fortified appearance similar to that of the palaces of fifteenth-century Florence, though the scale was much smaller.[6]

A massive, heavy door was placed in the center of the house front, with a smaller door at one side for personal use. Horse-drawn carriages passed through the larger gateway and a long, high corridor called a *zaguán*. This passageway led in turn to an open courtyard where passengers descended. Beyond a decorative garden-patio, in reality an outdoor living room, was a smaller courtyard leading to offices and stables, kitchen and servants' quarters. The *zaguán*, central to this house plan, became a primary architectural expression in Mexican building and filtered northward until it fused with the similar Classical Revival central hall found in Tucson after 1880.[7]

Climate, materials, and building tradition stimulated the continuance of the patio form, but, like the houses themselves, patios lost refinement and formal dimensions as builders imported the plan to the northern frontier. Thus the open area became essentially a cooling air well, sheltered by extensive planting from the intensity of the summer sun.[8] Nevertheless the urban pattern of Spanish-Mexican life did extend north into present-day Arizona. Mexican Tucson was made up of low-profile, flush-front rectangular cluster houses built on a single level. The sun-dried-adobe brick buildings had packed mud floors and few window or door openings. Saguaro ribs or ocotillo stalks, laid at right angles and called *savinas*, covered the beamed ceilings; sometimes these were shirted over with *manta*, or unbleached muslin. Above the ceilings were flat mud roofs. Roof drains, called *canales*, pierced the exterior walls, tilting downward to drain rain water away from the perishable adobe. Such contiguous-wall structures protected one another from the elements and tempered the extreme desert temperatures.[9]

3

A special adaptation of this style was used in the presidio or walled town of Tucson. Hilario Gallego, a native, described it in 1926:

> There was a connected chain of little one-room houses all around the inside of the wall that had been built for the soldiers and their families and a few other people. The houses had openings for doorways and some of them had doors. A few had openings for windows, but most of them didn't even have holes for light; they were built just like a storehouse. Some of the doors were made of branches and sahuaro sticks tied together with twigs or . . . with rawhide. Sometimes the whole door . . . and windows were of rawhide.[10]

In the Mexican countryside a rural house developed which recalled the urban residence in that it too was built around a plaza or patio. This *hacienda* house from the start was a looser and more flexible form than its city counterpart, and on the Sonoran frontier it became simpler and looser still. The Sonoran *hacienda* repeated the mass and geometric simplicity of earlier houses, with flat façade, a *zaguán*, and small grilled windows. Behind it, and enclosed with a wall, were numerous dependencies — a belled chapel, a school, stores and workshops, and quarters for the personnel of the ranch.[11]

Modified on the frontier, the urban and *hacienda* house forms became fused in the architectural vernacular of the region by the end of the Mexican period in the Southwest. The first Anglo-Americans settled in the area now comprising southern Arizona shortly before it passed under the jurisdiction of the United States by the Gadsden Purchase, ratified in the summer of 1854. These settlers, however, did little building, nor were they numerous enough, even by the end of the decade, to begin to adapt the regional architecture to their own purposes. Not until the tide of immigration into southern Arizona increased after the Civil War did any significant fusion of American with Spanish-Mexican architectural forms occur.

The change in architecture resulting from the Anglo-American migration between 1865 and 1880 was most evident in Tucson. Mrs. Granville H. Oury, a bride from the deep South, described the town a few months after the close of the Civil War as "certainly the most forlorn, dreary, desolate, God forsaken spot of earth ever trodden by the foot of a white man." Architecture was still purely Mexican; eleven years of United States sovereignty had left no visible mark on the face of the village. "The low, mud hovels are constructed regardless of comfort or convenience," Mrs. Oury noted with distaste; "there are but one or two glass windows in the town and not a single board floor. [There are] narrow, crooked, filthy streets, [and] very few whitewashed walls."[12]

Fifteen years later Tucson presented a very changed appearance. Alongside the contiguous-room, flat-roofed adobe characteristic of the Mexican frontier, there appeared the detached building, still with adobe walls, but with a pyramidal roof of wood shingles or sheet metal. A wide flowing roof covered porches on the front and sometimes on all sides of the house. Thick walls, a central hall reminiscent of the Spanish *zaguán*, and high ceilings created an aura of elegance, while extended eaves protected the exterior walls, doors, and windows from desert sun and the elements. At the same time the flat roofs of existing adobes were often covered with gable or hipped shingle roofs as Mexican tradition gave way to the "newness that was goodness" of the eastern United States. The fusion of the two traditions, the one Spanish-Mexican and the other Anglo-American, had created a house type that was technically and aesthetically ideal.

Architectural change was further accelerated by completion of the Southern Pacific Railroad through southern Arizona in 1880. Cheap railway freight rates now permitted the importation of building supplies from all areas of the nation, so that, for the first time, the Southwest was not dependent on indigenous materials. From Eastern centers of culture and commerce, carpenter-copy and mail-order catalogues flooded the region, even as travelers and settlers brought new ideas of refinement and elegance. The result was the rapid development of new canons of taste, and this in turn led to massive architectural borrowing all over the West.[13]

In Tucson an efflorescence of Victorian architecture began well before 1885, buttressed by the extensive use of wood for exterior trim and ornamentation. Two-story brick buildings with classical cornices adorned the town's business district, vying in elegance with Greek Revival false fronts added to the adobe carcasses of the original buildings.[14] The revolution in domestic buildings was no less conspicuous. An elegant frame-and-adobe residence, for instance, was built for Thomas Fitch, attorney, legislator, and orator. Two stories in height and topped with a Second-Empire mansard roof, the structure had bay windows in front and large, classically arched windows above, which bespoke a greater regard for style than for protection against summer temperatures. Tucson's indigenous architecture persisted, especially among the poor, completely overshadowed but by no means eliminated. "In some adobe, dirty house," said a contemporary commentator, "two or three Mexican families huddle together in mire and muck," just as they had always done, regardless of Mr. Fitch's palace across the way.[15]

An important element in the economy of Anglo-American Arizona as it evolved after the Civil War was the Territory's new cattle industry. As early as the end of the seventeenth century, Spanish missionaries had introduced domestic cattle into the settlements of peaceful Indians in northern Sonora and southern Arizona, and beef herds had played an important part in making the missions self-sufficient.[16] Subsequently both the Spanish Crown

The development of the Territorial Southern Arizona ranch house.

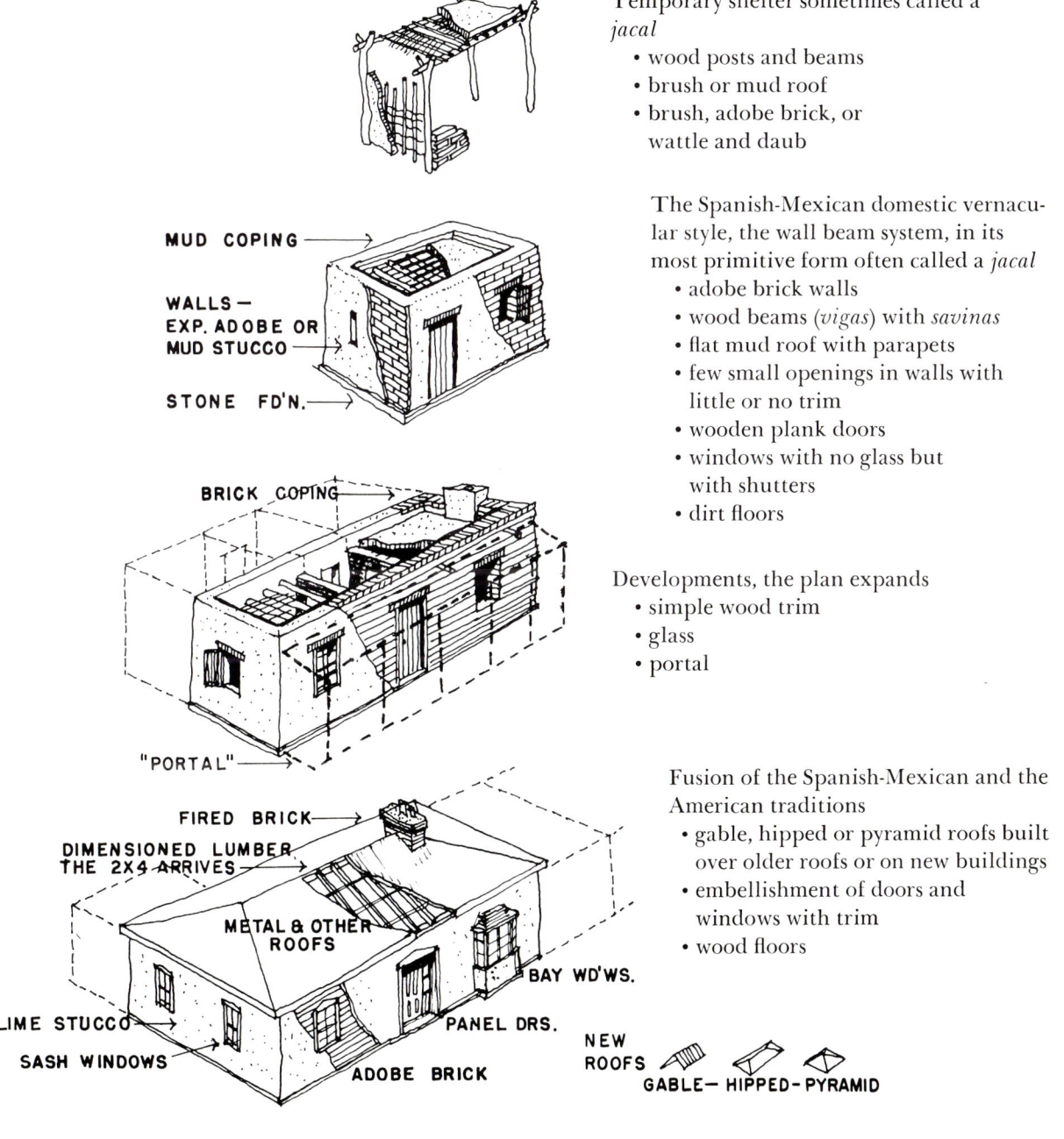

Temporary shelter sometimes called a *jacal*
- wood posts and beams
- brush or mud roof
- brush, adobe brick, or wattle and daub

MUD COPING

WALLS—
EXP. ADOBE OR
MUD STUCCO

STONE FD'N.

The Spanish-Mexican domestic vernacular style, the wall beam system, in its most primitive form often called a *jacal*
- adobe brick walls
- wood beams (*vigas*) with *savinas*
- flat mud roof with parapets
- few small openings in walls with little or no trim
- wooden plank doors
- windows with no glass but with shutters
- dirt floors

BRICK COPING

"PORTAL"

Developments, the plan expands
- simple wood trim
- glass
- portal

FIRED BRICK

DIMENSIONED LUMBER
THE 2X4 ARRIVES

METAL & OTHER
ROOFS

BAY WD'WS.

LIME STUCCO

SASH WINDOWS

PANEL DRS.

ADOBE BRICK

NEW
ROOFS

GABLE— HIPPED- PYRAMID

Fusion of the Spanish-Mexican and the American traditions
- gable, hipped or pyramid roofs built over older roofs or on new buildings
- embellishment of doors and windows with trim
- wood floors

and the Mexican government gave land grants covering thousands of acres to individuals, and much of the land thus given was used for ranching. By the beginning of the nineteenth century, the northwestern frontier of New Spain was the site of a viable and prosperous cattle industry.[17] But raiding by hostile Apaches after the Mexican War of Independence (1821) forced the frontier to contract and, like other settlers, ranchers abandoned their holdings, retreating southward toward security in Mexico. By the late 1840s, when the first sizeable number of Anglo-Americans penetrated the far Southwest on their way to the California gold fields, the principal evidences of the Spanish-Mexican cattle industry were abandoned ranches and vast herds of wild cattle.

The gold rush in California brought thousands of immigrants from all over the country before the end of the 1840s, and thereby created a demand for food which the region could not meet. The situation was aggravated after 1851 by a great drought, which worsened an already bad situation.[18] This crisis persuaded a few enterprising men to run the risks of Indian depredations and natural calamities and drive cattle herds from as far east as Arkansas across the Southwest to the Pacific coast. Some Arizonans attempted to build herds by capturing and breeding strays. A handful of others, including Granville Oury's brother William, drove their own herds into Arizona. These efforts were sporadic, however, and ranching remained small-scale. The coming of the Civil War in 1861 forced the withdrawal of federal troops from the region. Apache raiding resumed with greater ferocity than ever, driving nearly all Americans out of the Gadsden Purchase area. "The Apaches swept out from the hills and, along with Mexican bandits, desolated ranch after ranch until no man's life was safe," said Sylvester Mowry. Desolation "was never so sudden and so complete." The cattle industry collapsed. Near the end of the war

8

William S. Oury drove the first herd of superior cattle into Arizona when he brought his daughter from school in St. Louis.[19]

In the postwar years Anglo-Americans immigrated to Arizona in increasing numbers, many lured by the prospect of mineral wealth. With them came the army, whose task it was to subdue the Apaches and other hostile Indians and make the new Territory safe for white occupation. By 1869 there were some two thousand troops stationed at fourteen posts in Arizona, and citizens continually demanded additional forces, claiming that the military still failed to give them adequate protection. The result was a constant increase in troop levels until, by the end of the Apache wars in the mid-1880s, nearly one half of all the line troops in the army were stationed in the Military Department of Arizona.[20]

The task of feeding the army called Arizona's postwar cattle industry into being. In August of 1866, Henry C. Hooker, formerly a merchant in Placerville, California, came to the Territory, and the following year procured cattle which he furnished on contract to the garrison at Camp Crittenden, in southern Arizona. His affairs prospered, and by the early 1870s he claimed a dominant position among the stockmen of the Territory. In 1872 alone, with his partner Hugh Hinds, he purchased and drove into Arizona four herds of Texas cattle totaling 15,500 head.[21] In February of that year he established the Sierra Bonita Ranch in the rich grazing lands of the Sulphur Springs Valley south of the Gila River. Hooker's partners in this enterprise were William B. Hooper, the head of a prosperous and important San Francisco mercantile house, and his associate, James M. Barney, the most influential businessman of Yuma. The firm of William B. Hooper and Company was deeply involved in furnishing goods and services to the government, and claimed the largest share of contracts for the Indian service in Arizona.[22]

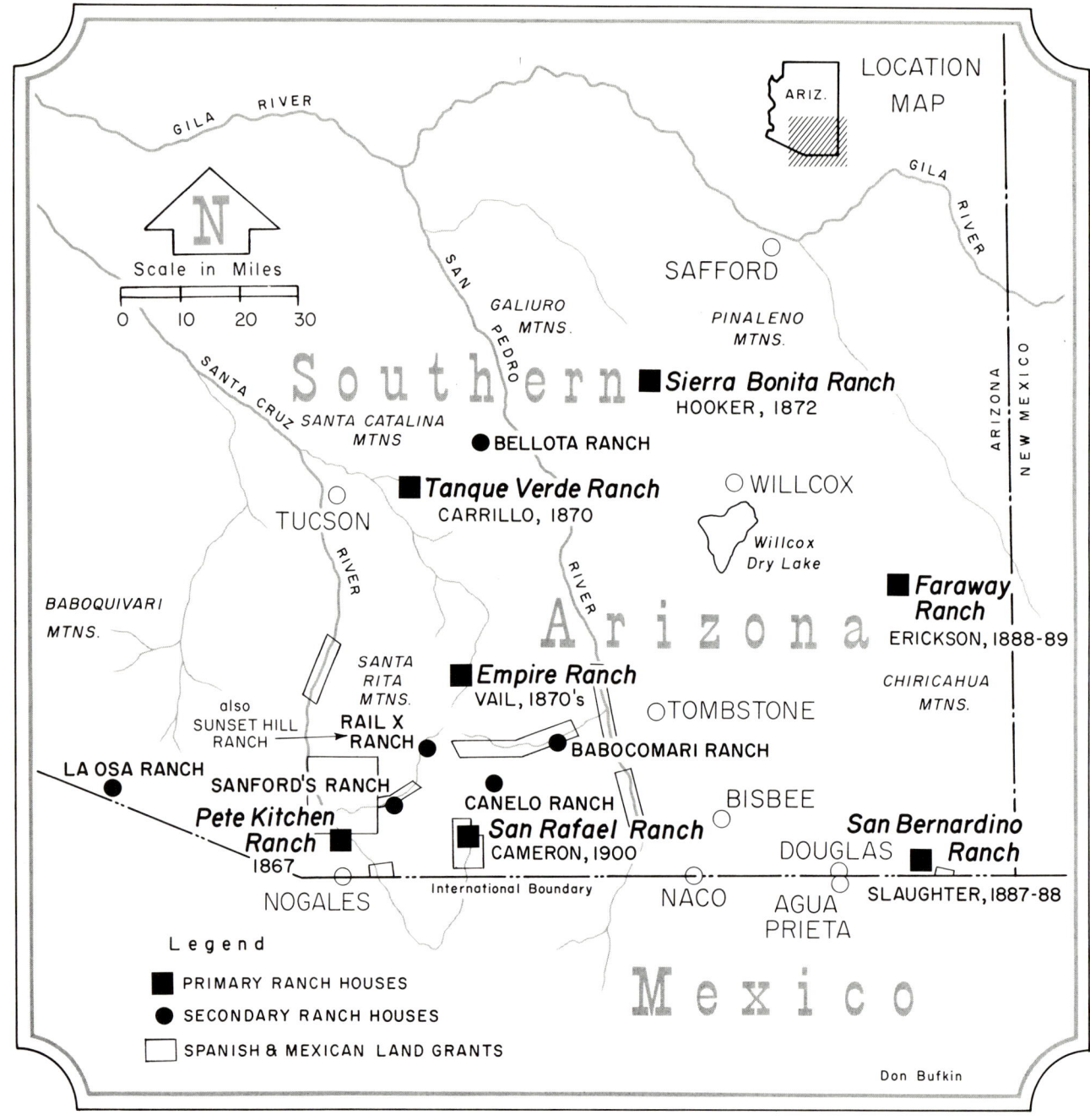

LOCATION MAP

ARIZ.

GILA RIVER

N
Scale in Miles
0   10   20   30

GILA RIVER

SAFFORD

GALIURO MTNS.

PINALENO MTNS.

ARIZONA / NEW MEXICO

Southern

SAN PEDRO

SANTA CRUZ

SANTA CATALINA MTNS

BELLOTA RANCH

■ *Sierra Bonita Ranch*
HOOKER, 1872

○ WILLCOX

■ *Tanque Verde Ranch*
CARRILLO, 1870

TUCSON

RIVER

Willcox Dry Lake

BABOQUIVARI MTNS.

Arizona

RIVER

■ *Faraway Ranch*
ERICKSON, 1888-89

CHIRICAHUA MTNS.

also SUNSET HILL RANCH

SANTA RITA MTNS.

RAIL X RANCH

■ *Empire Ranch*
VAIL, 1870's

○ TOMBSTONE

BABOCOMARI RANCH

LA OSA RANCH

SANFORD'S RANCH

CANELO RANCH

BISBEE

Pete Kitchen Ranch
1867

■ San Rafael Ranch
CAMERON, 1900

DOUGLAS

■ *San Bernardino Ranch*
SLAUGHTER, 1887-88

NOGALES

International Boundary

NACO

AGUA PRIETA

Mexico

Legend
■ PRIMARY RANCH HOUSES
● SECONDARY RANCH HOUSES
☐ SPANISH & MEXICAN LAND GRANTS

Don Bufkin

The Sierra Bonita did well from the beginning. Less than a year and a half after its establishment, Hooker had about four thousand head of horned cattle and a thousand calves on his lands, in addition to a sizeable herd of saddle horses, brood mares, and stallions. A pioneer in scientific breeding (along with Colin Cameron), he early imported shorthorn, Durham, and Hereford stock; as soon thereafter as he could do so, he purged his herds of all Mexican or Texan animals.[23] After 1879 he bought no more cattle, but simply depended upon the increase of his herds to fill mounting orders from the army and Indian service for beef and from other cattlemen for blooded stock. Despite heavy losses during an Apache outbreak from the San Carlos reservation in the autumn of 1881, he continued to do business with the government. By early in 1884, he could look back on nearly two decades as a government contractor or sub-contractor, during which he had furnished more than 100,000 head of beef and stock cattle.[24]

Henry Hooker's rise as a cattleman was unique in Arizona, but the industry he led prospered as he did. Throughout the Territory there were excellent grazing lands with a seemingly inexhaustible supply of sacaton, grama, and other nutritive grasses. Homesteading was easy, and ranchers encountered little difficulty in appropriating public lands for their use. Abundant capital was available, both in the East and abroad, for investment in cattle ranching.[25] The growth of towns and cities, and the constant increase in Arizona's population, provided dependable local markets for beef raised in the Territory, and the expansion of army and Indian-service activity through the mid-1880s gave promise of continuing government contracts. Finally, the construction of two transcontinental railroads through Arizona between 1880 and 1883 furnished easy and economical access to marketplaces in all parts of the country.[26]

The decade of the 1870s saw a great proliferation of cattle-ranching operations in southern Arizona. Most were small, on limited range and with herds numbering no more than a few hundred head, but a few, such as the Vail brothers' Empire Ranch southeast of Tucson, ultimately covered a thousand square miles and supported huge herds. The following decade saw the pattern of expansion continue and spread into northern Arizona, where the coming of the Santa Fe Railroad stimulated the development of the Mogollon Rim country.[27]

Overstocking of Arizona's cattle ranges had begun before the end of the 1870s, although ranchers, still contemplating a future of endless prosperity, failed to recognize the fact. With herds already at optimum size, a mass influx of Texas cattle occurred, brought by ranchers who had left the state after passage, in 1879, of land laws calling for payment of leasing fees for use of state lands.[28] Shortly thereafter, renewed drought in California caused cattlemen there to drive their stock into the valleys of western Arizona, to find the forage and water their native range no longer afforded.[29]

Even as these incursions took place, the land was becoming progressively less able to sustain the burden of additional cattle. Although a few far-seeing ranchers had worked to improve their ranges, experimenting with new grasses and better methods of water dispersion, the quality of most grazing lands had declined severely. In part this deterioration was due to the harvesting of wild grasses by enterprising contractors for sale to the army as hay; repeated and frequent cuttings had destroyed the plants. Far more, however, the damage resulted from overgrazing by larger numbers of animals than the regional ecology could sustain. The inevitable destruction of range grasses was followed by increased erosion, and the land, without a stable ground cover to retain moisture, dried more rapidly than before, thus damaging the grasses still more.

The deterioration of the pasturelands was signalized in the increasing invasion of mesquite growth on areas previously rich with grass.[30]

By the mid-1880s it was clear to many observers that Arizona's cattle ranges were overstocked, and that they were becoming progressively less able to support even the number of animals which previously had been optimum. Other problems from outside the Territory also bedeviled cattlemen. The vast expansion of ranching from Texas to Montana had produced more beef than national markets could absorb; the glut drove prices down and forced small producers out of business all over the West. To combat adverse marketing pressures, and belatedly to attempt range improvement, many Arizona ranchers banded together in large companies. Ranching thus entered a corporate phase which promised greater success in scientific breeding and the bettering of grazing conditions than individual efforts in the past had achieved. But the cattle companies failed to limit the size of herds, and overpopulation of the ranges was increased after disastrous snows during the winter of 1886–1887 had crippled ranching on the Great Plains as far south as Texas.[31]

Cattle ranching in Arizona reached a peak in 1891. In that year, the annual tax census of animals on the ranges revealed 720,940 head, but probably twice that number actually were being supported within the Territory. The same year saw the beginning of an intense drought which soon threatened the very existence of the industry. By the early summer of 1892 there was very little water and virtually no grass on the ranges, and cattlemen desperately shipped thousands of animals outside Arizona to prevent their starving. The number of cattle which died of malnutrition and thirst was nevertheless staggering. By July of 1893, when the rains finally came again, ranchers in the southern part of the Territory

A round-up on the San Pedro near Hereford, before the arid years of the early 90s.

had lost between fifty and seventy-five per cent of their animals. It was estimated that, had the drought continued until the end of that year, the surviving remnant of the herds would have perished as well.[32]

The crisis of 1891–1893 taught Arizona cattlemen a lesson which they could have learned by no other means. Throughout the rest of the decade, they devoted their energies to fencing and improving their ranges, limiting the size of their herds, and upgrading the quality of their stock. By 1900 the focus of territorial ranching was primarily on breeding superior animals rather than on feeding large herds. Before the end of the territorial period in 1912, improved range and carefully limited use of the public domain (for which stockmen now were obliged to pay grazing fees) permitted the gradual expansion of herds again. Ranching thus survived as a viable and significant part of Arizona's economy.[33]

14

As the homes of some of the wealthiest and most prominent Arizonans of the late nineteenth century, territorial ranch houses have an importance all their own. Through them the perceptive visitor or scholar can reclaim a segment of history now past, and sense its challenges and opportunities, its tastes and mores. As architectural monuments, however, they can claim even more significance, for they demonstrate an unbroken chain of evolution extending from the Spanish-Mexican vernacular to the high Victorian development in the rural house.

Between the ranch house which Pete Kitchen built on Potrero Creek, north of present-day Nogales, in 1867 and the mansion erected for Colin Cameron at San Rafael on the border in 1900, there existed a world of difference in comfort, security, and refinement. Less than ten years of building covered the development from the Spanish-Mexican strip house through the house built in an L shape — which suggested development of the patio plan — to the erection of the full *hacienda* house as epitomized in Hooker's Sierra Bonita (1872). By the mid-1880s the trend of building had moved away from the native vernacular, and significant differences appeared. Neil Erickson's Faraway Ranch was a two-storied structure, built of wood and stone as well as adobe, and it had a pitched roof. Nevertheless, like earlier houses, it grew by addition to earlier, existing structures. The final gesture of independence from the native tradition was visible in the San Bernardino Ranch of John H. Slaughter, which was built "all of a piece" and had a distinctively Anglo-American profile and quality. San Rafael completed the evolutionary picture, bringing luxury and graciousness unknown in earlier Arizona houses, and bespeaking a land finally tamed and an industry at last settled.

Frontier Fortresses

The Kitchen home on the Potrero, 1915.

Pete Kitchen's Ranch

Tanque Verde

Built within five years of each other, Pete Kitchen's ranch house on Potrero Creek and the house Emilio Carrillo built as headquarters for his Tanque Verde ranch east of Tucson epitomized the Spanish-Mexican frontier style. Each was constructed on a simple pattern varying only slightly from the urban strip house consisting of a row of adobe rooms. The attached ells suggested the need for a patio or outdoor area where some security was possible against attackers. The imperatives of defense, indeed, went far toward determining the location and plan of both houses.

Pete Kitchen, a lean, tough Kentuckian, came to Arizona in the 1850s, farmed for a few years along the Santa Cruz River, started supplying the military forces with beef, and eventually became superintendent for Grant and Taliaferro, government contractors.[1]

In 1867 he began building his adobe ranch house in the upper Santa Cruz Valley, long before military campaigning had done more than suggest an eventual end to the menace of Apache hostility. The valley was a prime trail for marauders heading for Mexico, and the stretch of country between Tucson and Magdalena reportedly was the bloodiest for hundreds of miles around.

17

Apaches passed the Kitchen ranch going both south and north, and frequently attacked stock and herders unlucky or unwise enough to leave themselves exposed. Kitchen trained his Mexican and Opata ranch hands in defense tactics, however, and stayed in business.

To his herd of 700 Mexican cattle, brought in from Sonora, he added a drove of hogs for the Tucson market, where "Pete Kitchen hams" became a welcome variation from Mexican beans. His pork products were transported to points as far away as Silver City, New Mexico, and his hogs were famous all over the Southwest. Like Kitchen, they were often in danger from Indian attacks.[2] Yet despite numerous depredations which cost Pete heavy losses in stock, the lives of many of his ranch hands, and even the murder of an adopted son, the rancher refused to abandon his lands and home.[3] He survived the era of Apache hostility, selling out in 1883 after the coming of the railroad had made his large truck-gardening operation no longer profitable in southern Arizona.[4]

Built upon a hill overlooking a thousand acres of arable land, Pete Kitchen's house was a prime example of a desert stronghold-fortress. The dwelling consisted of four rooms, of which three were built contiguously on a north-south line, while a fourth projected westward from the northern end of the house. The roof was flat with a surrounding parapet three to four feet in height. Here in times of attack Kitchen, his Mexican wife Rosa, and his Opata ranch hands could lie in relative security, shooting through loopholes pierced in the wall but safe from the Indians' return fire. At such times Doña Rosa gathered guns from their wall racks, twisted her skirts about her legs in Oriental fashion for easy movement and fired her weapons along with the hands. On hot summer nights in peaceful times, the roof provided sleeping room for the family.[5]

The Kitchen house, 1973, from the southeast. The north and south wings are later additions.

West of the house, a patio was formed by extension of the ell, and a wall enclosed a small amount of land beyond it. Here was a well, dug by hand to a depth of sixty feet, which supplied water to the household. Against the west wall of the house were adobe steps leading to the roof, but these unquestionably were an addition dating from the time after Indian troubles had ended; no frontiersman in an exposed position would have offered the enemy such ready access to his last redoubt. Rather, Kitchen, his family, and his men must have mounted by a ladder or ladders which they could pull up behind them.[6]

Outside the patio wall were the dependencies of the ranch house: an adobe building providing quarters for employees, smoke houses in which hams and sides of bacon were cured, vats for rendering lard, and the corrals where beef cattle, horses, and mules could be held against Apache attempts to stampede and run them off. Here too, probably, were the shops where artisans kept wagons and harness in repair for the long trips which Kitchen and his family often made to markets in Tucson and elsewhere. Finally, there was a commissary building where employees drew supplies, a courtesy also extended to destitute travelers fortunate enough to pass by the ranch.[7]

The walls of the Kitchen ranch house were massive. Twenty-one inches thick, they acted to conserve heat during the winters and to keep the house cool in the hot months, and they also provided a good defense against attack. Only the southern and central rooms had windows, but, being sixty-three inches in length, they were far larger than was common in houses of that era and place and thus constituted a distinctive architectural feature of the structure. Within, the rooms fronting the house were spacious — fifteen feet wide, with beamed ceilings fourteen feet high. Floors were of packed earth. Two fireplaces, one in the center chamber, the other

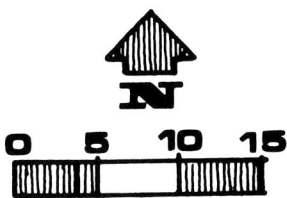

0   5   10   15

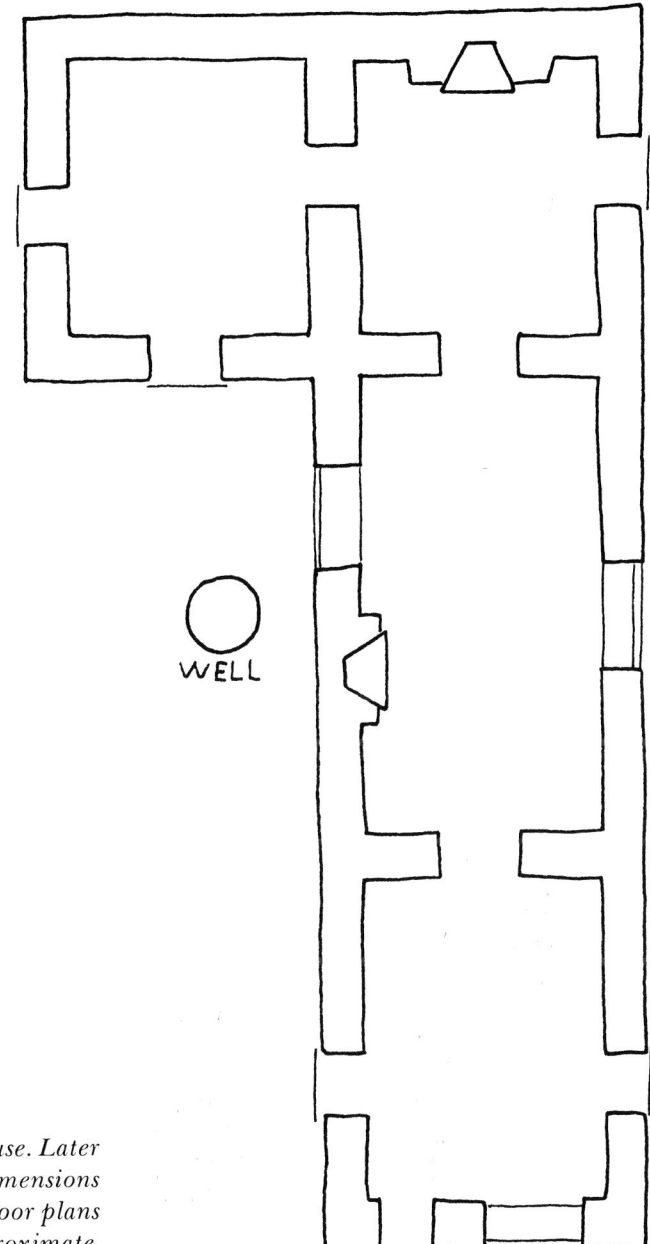

WELL

Pete Kitchen's original ranch house. Later additions are not included. The dimensions for this and the following floor plans are approximate.

21

The Pete Kitchen dining room.

in the room to the north, provided heat during the winter, while the latter also was used for cooking. The northern end of the house furnished space for living functions, while sleeping quarters for the family were in the south room.[8]

Since Kitchen's occupancy, many alterations have been made. In 1900 floors of poured concrete replaced the original dirt surface. At the same time, a shake-shingled hipped roof was erected above the flat adobe, but a later owner, Colonel Gilbert Proctor, removed this monument to Anglo taste, restoring the flat roof and parapet when he acquired the property in 1947. Already, the wall dividing the southern from the central room had been removed, making a single, large and imposing chamber whose dimensions and simplicity today recall some of the early Spanish mission churches in New Mexico. Perhaps at the same time as this alteration, a third fireplace was built, this one in the southernmost wall of the house. In 1943 the original cottonwood ceiling beams were replaced with square-hewn pine timbers. Four years later, Colonel Proctor enlarged the house, adding an ell to the northeast to balance the original westward extension. At the same time he also built onto the southern end of the house and added a long covered porch, or *portal*, with tiled roof and floor, along the eastern façade. Until his death in 1972, Proctor used the house as an Indian museum as well as a residence.[9]

Tanque Verde

Emilio Carrillo, a native of Sonora, began ranching at the foot of Tanque Verde Ridge east of Tucson in 1870, moving from Rillito Creek to take up lands there. His choice was wise.[10] The surrounding country, well watered, rose toward the base of the

23

Rincon Mountains to the southeast but opened into lush grazing lands farther south and west. Already William Oury had brought his herd of blooded Kentucky cattle to the area and had done well despite the menace of recurrent Indian raids. Tanque Verde offered good possibilities for defense, and the richness of the land afforded opportunities to the enterprising rancher prepared to take the risks necessary to exploit them.

Carrillo built his house in typical Sonoran style on a rise backing up, on the east side, to the base of the ridge. Its plan was modest and simple. Like Kitchen's ranch house, the L-shaped structure followed the Spanish-Mexican tradition. The house comprised three rooms only, two built contiguously on a north-south axis, and the third forming an ell at the north end, facing east. The construction was of adobe, massive and unornamented. A flat roof, surrounded by a parapet wall, perhaps anticipated the needs of defense, but Carrillo added a distinctive touch to this utilitarian

Tanque Verde. Additions indicate its use as a guest ranch.

This was Carrillo's bedroom. The saguaro-rib ceiling is original.

purpose by planting the earthen surface with barley as was the custom in Sonora. The grass provided good additional insulation against summer heat, and might retard fire as well.[11]

Within, the demands of defense were apparent. Only two small windows and a single iron-bolted door pierced the western façade, which overlooked the open valley; from this direction Indian attack probably would come. To the north, east, and south there was no fenestration. At two places on each exterior wall, however, gun ports cut through. These holes, mere slits on the outside, widened sharply within the walls, so as to give the greatest possible latitude of fire to the defender within. Carrillo's house, no less than Kitchen's, was a fortress.

The exterior walls measured twenty-three inches in width, and the wall dividing the northern and southern rooms was just as thick. Doors were of heavy wood, hung on iron hinges and secured with massive bolts. Ceilings, made of saguaro ribs laid on top of exposed rounded beams or *vigas*, reached a height of eleven feet. In the southern room, the shorter of the two on line, a major central round supporting beam ran the length of the ceiling below the *vigas*. The reason for this architectural anomaly is unclear, since neither of the other rooms had any comparable feature, but it may have indicated a weakness or defect in the walls, necessitating further support for the heavy roof.

Although smaller than Kitchen's, Carrillo's house had a luxury which the larger residence lacked — as did most other Arizona homes of the period. His bedroom had a wooden floor laid with six-inch pine boards hand-sawed from trees cut by ranch employees on the adjoining Rincon Mountains. Although lumbering had been carried on in southern Arizona since before the Civil War, one local tradition maintains that this was the earliest wooden floor in the region. True or not, it was a rare refinement on the remote Southwestern frontier.[12]

The floor of the north room, devoted to family and business matters, was of packed dirt and was covered with rushes that were watered down each morning for cooling and dust control. The original windows, heavily shuttered, were closed in the daytime to keep out the rays of the blistering sun and the desert heat.

The east room of the Tanque Verde ranch house served as a kitchen for Carrillo and his family. Outside, the south wall of this ell gave access to the patio through a single door in the east wall of the house. The patio provided sleeping room for the ranch hands in all but the worst weather; during severe storms they crowded into a small adobe hut, which Carrillo had occupied at the time the house was being constructed. Within the patio, and against the east wall of the house, there was an adobe fireplace where food for the employees was prepared. Carrillo followed Spanish-Mexican custom in placing some of his cooking arrangements out of doors.

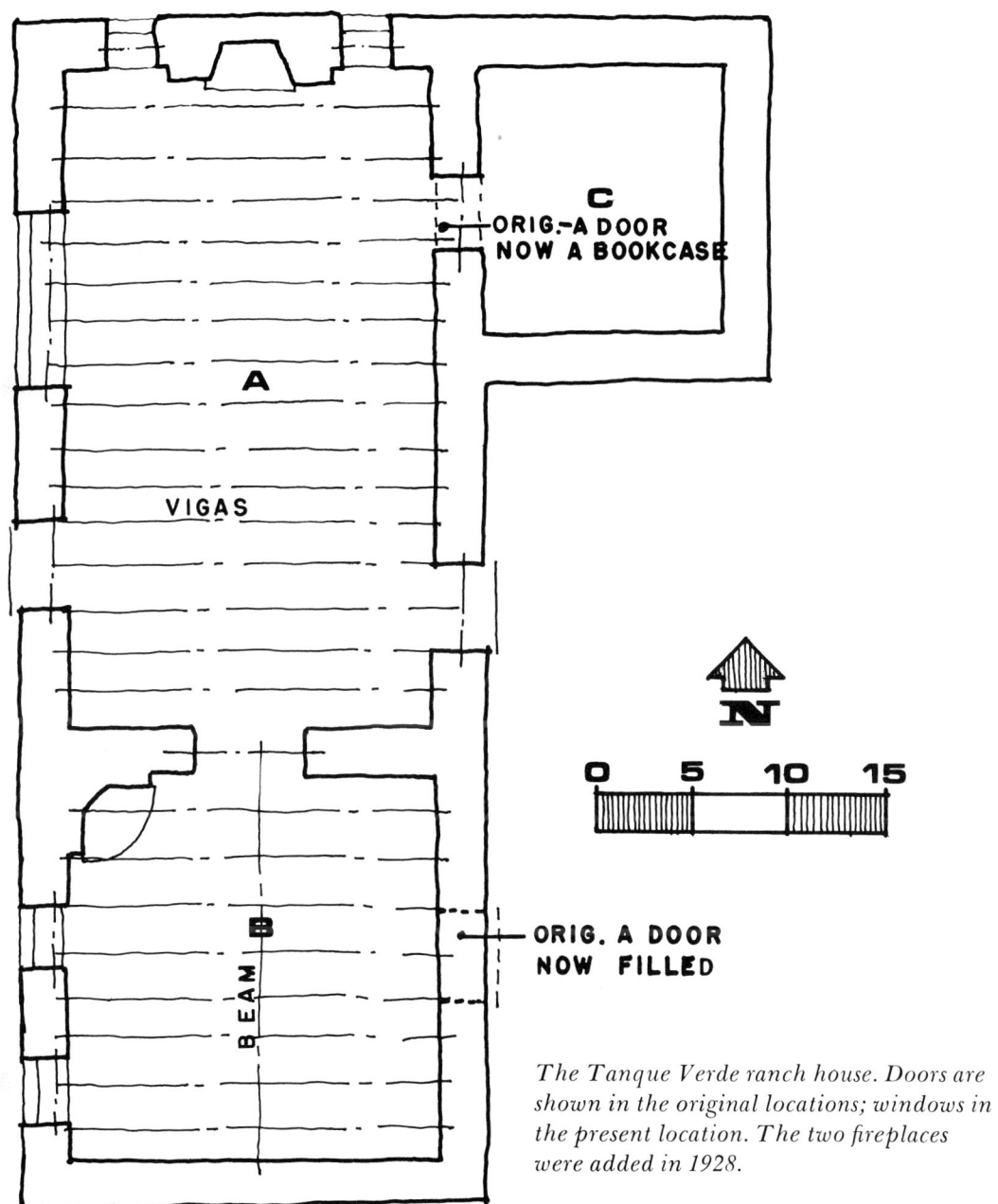

C

ORIG.-A DOOR
NOW A BOOKCASE

A

VIGAS

N

0 5 10 15

BEAM B

ORIG. A DOOR
NOW FILLED

The Tanque Verde ranch house. Doors are shown in the original locations; windows in the present location. The two fireplaces were added in 1928.

27

There was no well, but three springs rose nearby, and the flow from one of them Carrillo diverted to pass through the patio and into the house, thus providing a continual source of fresh, running water. Beyond the outer patio wall were the ranch corrals, made from double mesquite posts and interwoven branches, where up to four hundred head of cattle could be held. The proximity of the corrals to the house and patio assured that Indians and rustlers would be unable to make off with the herd without alerting Carrillo and his men. Nearby were the gardens which provided the ranch with fresh produce, as well as a surplus which could be marketed in Tucson. Finally, at the springs, Carrillo had his men make the adobe bricks used in the construction of the ranch house and outbuildings.[13]

All his care in building for defense did not secure him from attack. He was known to have large sums of money hidden in the house, and in 1904 bandits overpowered Carrillo's men, put a rope around his neck, threw it over the bedroom beam, and started raising him to make him tell where his money was. He did not betray his hiding place, which was under the hearth of the massive kitchen stove — $85,000 in gold — but he never recovered from the shock of the attack.[14]

The Tanque Verde ranch house has undergone extensive alterations since it was built. The original windows were walled up and other, larger ones were cut. The defensive gun ports have also disappeared — the token of a safer age. About 1900, Carrillo's son Rafael bowed to the prevailing architectural taste and replaced the flat roof with a low and massive gabled one, covered with galvanized iron brought by the new railroad. The additional space he gained thereby was used for a storage garret, which was reached by an outside wooden stairway. When James Converse, a later owner, tried to remove this roof in order to restore the original silhouette

The massive walls (twenty-three inches thick) typify the Mexican style and fortress-like adobe construction of Tanque Verde.

29

The temporary shelter, dating from about 1870, where Carrillo lived during the construction of the ranch headquarters.

of the house, he found the task impossible, so well had the addition been constructed.

In 1928 Tanque Verde became a guest ranch, and this new use led to further modifications, as well as enlargement, of the house. The east room was expanded to provide space for better kitchen facilities. Interior fireplaces were added. The west wall was shored up with a stone-and-mortar border projecting eight inches above and eighteen inches below ground; desert rats and squirrels had severely damaged the original foundations. Converse also added a *portal* with a brick floor to the western façade of the house. Finally, he built a large addition to the north. This new structure, also of adobe, carried on the idiom of the old ranch house in that it returned to the flat roof and raised parapet, while the *portal* fronting it added further appearance of architectural uniformity.[15]

Both the Kitchen and Tanque Verde ranch houses now serve purposes very different from those for which they were built. Gone are the dangers from Indian and outlaw; gone, too, the original functions of the ranches over which their proud and enterprising owners watched. But passing time and changing circumstances have not diminished the appropriateness of these two houses to the region. Indeed, the facility with which each was adapted to new functions underlines the conclusion that both structures embody singularly efficient, as well as pleasing, solutions to the problems of desert design.

The Regional Style Matures

The Sierra Bonita — Mexican architecture at maturity.

Sierra Bonita

WITH THE CONSTRUCTION of Henry C. Hooker's Sierra Bonita ranch house, begun in 1872, Spanish-Mexican domestic architecture in Arizona achieved its highest development. Other houses were built on a simple plan; the Sierra Bonita was a fully articulated country *hacienda*. The homes of other ranchers mirrored lives of hardship and danger, in which most of the amenities were sacrificed to the sovereign aim of survival. From the time of its construction, Hooker's house bespoke a graciousness reminiscent of his New England origin and entirely foreign to the Southwestern frontier.[1] Still more, it declared the refined taste of a man already wealthy and successful and conscious of the importance his prominence lent him. Elegantly furnished and boasting the most modern conveniences, the Sierra Bonita afforded every comfort to its owner, his family, and his guests. In this way, commented one traveler somewhat ruefully, it was "in striking contrast with the common ranch house of the range, that is minus every luxury and often barely furnishes the necessities of life."[2]

Hooker's ranch house was built around a long, rectangular courtyard, or patio. The three-sided structure followed the *hacienda* plan precisely; the fourth side of the quadrangle was enclosed

33

by a wall, beyond which stood some of the many dependencies of the ranch. The exterior walls of the house were sixteen feet high and twenty inches thick, the width of a double row of adobe bricks. For purposes of drainage, the roof, although almost flat, inclined toward the patio. A low parapet surrounded all three segments of the house, anticipating the need for defense.[3] So also did the arrangement of exterior windows and doors. According to family tradition, the only openings in the house, as originally built, gave onto the patio, to which access from the outside was gained through a gate in the wall of the carriage courtyard. At the same time, narrow gun ports pierced the outer walls.[4] Economy in exterior fenestration was traditional in the architectural form, but the other features resulted from the location of the ranch. Situated in the northern Sulphur Springs Valley, the Sierra Bonita lay astride the trail most commonly used by White Mountain and other Apaches for raiding into Mexico. Hooker's house, like Kitchen's, had to be a bastion of defense.

A *portal* (with wooden floor) around three sides of the patio shielded windows from direct sunlight and lent an illusion of coolness and tranquility. The courtyard, however, offered more than living space; it contained a well and windmill, with a water-storage tower alongside. There also was a root cellar within the walls, sufficiently protected from the heat of the day that foods could be kept fresh for a considerable time. Thus, in the unlikely event of a sustained siege by hostile tribesmen, the house and courtyard together could provide all the necessities of life to the defenders.[5]

The interior of the house was spacious and elegant. Three bedrooms (the last reserved for Mrs. Hooker) and a parlor formed a line along the northeast side of the structure. The parlor, "cheerfully furnished" according to an 1877 newspaper account and closed off by folding doors, provided office space for Hooker and a

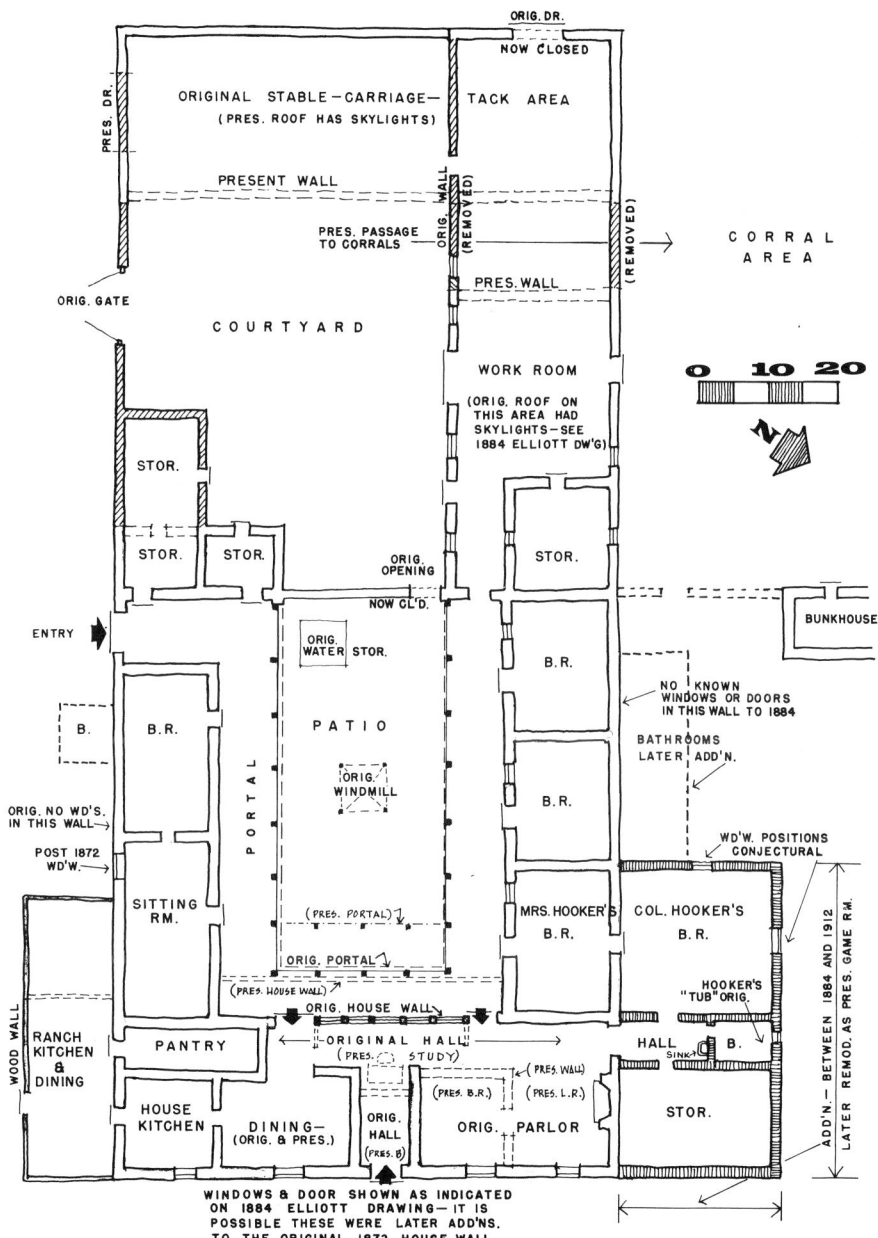

ORIG. DR.

NOW CLOSED

PRES. DR.

ORIGINAL STABLE – CARRIAGE –
(PRES. ROOF HAS SKYLIGHTS)

TACK AREA

PRESENT WALL

ORIG. WALL (REMOVED)

(REMOVED)

PRES. PASSAGE
TO CORRALS

PRES. WALL

CORRAL
AREA

ORIG. GATE

COURTYARD

WORK ROOM
(ORIG. ROOF ON
THIS AREA HAD
SKYLIGHTS – SEE
1884 ELLIOTT DW'G)

0   10   20

N

STOR.

STOR.   STOR.

ORIG.
OPENING

NOW CL'D.

STOR.

BUNKHOUSE

ENTRY

ORIG.
WATER STOR.

B.R.

NO KNOWN
WINDOWS OR DOORS
IN THIS WALL TO 1884

B.

B.R.

PATIO

ORIG. NO WD'S.
IN THIS WALL →

POST 1872
WD'W. →

ORIG.
WINDMILL

B.R.

BATHROOMS
LATER ADD'N.

WD'W. POSITIONS
CONJECTURAL

SITTING
RM.

(PRES. PORTAL)

MRS. HOOKER'S
B.R.

COL. HOOKER'S
B.R.

ORIG. PORTAL

(PRES. HOUSE WALL)

HOOKER'S
"TUB" ORIG.

ORIG. HOUSE WALL

ORIGINAL HALL

(PRES. STUDY)

(PRES. B.R.)

(PRES. WALL)

(PRES. L.R.)

HALL   B.

SINK

WOOD WALL

RANCH
KITCHEN
& DINING

PANTRY

HOUSE
KITCHEN

DINING
(ORIG. & PRES.)

ORIG.
HALL
(PRES. B)

ORIG. PARLOR

STOR.

ADD'N. – BETWEEN 1884 AND 1912
LATER REMOD. AS PRES. GAME RM.

WINDOWS & DOOR SHOWN AS INDICATED
ON 1884 ELLIOTT DRAWING – IT IS
POSSIBLE THESE WERE LATER ADD'NS.
TO THE ORIGINAL 1872 HOUSE WALL

*The Sierra Bonita
ranch house — the
1872 floor plan with
later changes indi-
cated, including alter-
ations after 1884 and
up to 1971.*

35

The present entry from the south.

gracious living room for his guests.[6] Adjoining Mrs. Hooker's room was the master's bedroom and adjacent to these rooms and the parlor was a bathroom which Hooker had equipped with the first Victorian scroll-foot bathtub in the valley. East of these retreats was the family dining room which in turn backed up to a long kitchen. Here meals for the family were prepared. An interior wall divided the kitchen from a large pantry, and both the pantry and the family kitchen opened on a second kitchen and dining room where the cowboys and other hired hands ate. This dining room occupied the end of the long wing of the house, and like the family kitchen and pantry did not open on the patio. Every major room in the house had a fireplace, Hooker being determined that everyone should be comfortable.[7]

At the other end of the house from Hooker's bedroom stood the workroom and storage room whose northeast corner touched the most westerly of the bedrooms. The adjacent stables included an architectural innovation. They were lighted by skylights as well as by doors opening on the patio. They provided space for seventeen horses, box stalls for stallions, and room for all the necessary harness and tack.[8]

The large and opulent Sierra Bonita ranch house was but the center of a complex of structures. Southwest of the house stood a huge adobe corral, capable — according to one contemporary account — of holding three thousand head of cattle.[9] Other corrals, both of adobe and of plank, held horses which ranch hands and members of the family needed for their daily tasks. Near these enclosures stood another architectural rarity for the Southwest: a barn built mostly of wood, with a gabled roof, and the legend "Sierra Bonita Ranch 1872" proudly lettered above the doors. Beyond, to the north, stood a large adobe-walled corral in which Hooker stored his hay — the best in the valley — safe from the stock which grazed the surrounding ranges.[10] The establishment also

The courtyard. At one time it contained a well, windmill and water tank.

included paddocks, a mill for grinding grains which the ranch produced, a blacksmith's shop, a large slaughterhouse, quarters for the forty-odd ranch hands whom Hooker employed, and a half-mile track where he worked the most promising of his race horses.[11]

The economy of the Sierra Bonita Ranch was highly diversified. Cattle raising was always its most important component; by the mid-1880s, more than 20,000 head of improved stock grazed its huge range, and there were upwards of five hundred acres under fence. The sale of blooded horses, raised both for saddle and for carriage use, also contributed importantly to income. Indeed, by 1884, Hooker was advertising his ranch as dealing in "cattle and horses of all grades."[12] Like most other early Southwestern ranches, the Sierra Bonita produced all the food consumed by its owner, his family, their guests, and the employees. There were large gardens, irrigated from two wells and by water from a ditch running across the Sulphur Springs Valley. A dairy herd guaranteed fresh milk and butter; a flock of poultry assured eggs and fowl for the table: a herd of hogs promised pork and bacon as highly prized alternatives to the beef which was the staple of every Arizonan's diet. Nor did Hooker, a renowned sportsman, neglect to furnish opportunities for the recreation of his guests. Two large ponds, dug to water range cattle, were stocked with German carp; the activity of the angler could also put onto the table a delicacy rare to the desert. Finally, for hunting, racing, and companionship, the rancher maintained a kennel of greyhounds.[13]

Hooker's holdings in land were large, and he kept expanding them. Beginning with a homestead of one hundred sixty acres, he ended by controlling a range which measured twenty miles west to east, and nearly thirty north to south. Most of this vast area was public domain which he was able to pre-empt for his use by virtue of early claims on its water sources. Control of water conferred a recognized right to adjacent lands. By 1884, however, Hooker held title not only to his home place but also to six ranches neighboring the Sierra Bonita. He put these properties to the same use as he did his original holdings, using them for agricultural and stock-raising purposes. The next year he also acquired Hooker Hot Springs in the Galiuro Mountains, one of the best known of Arizona's early resorts, and subsequently developed it both for tourists and for health seekers.[14]

Not only was the Sierra Bonita one of Arizona's most important cattle ranches; it also became one of the best-known places in the Territory. Hooker's hospitality, always formal and Eastern, was as lavish as his house was elegant. The ranch early became the focal point for the social activity of officers stationed at Fort Grant, about ten miles away, and its proprietor became the genial host of governmental officials, scientists, newspapermen, writers, artists, and other distinguished men as they passed through Arizona.[15] From the society at the Sierra Bonita, as well as from Fort Grant, the dramatist Augustus Thomas conceived several characters for his successful and popular play, *Arizona: A Drama in Four Acts,* first presented in New York in 1899. Action in the drama took place at the Sierra Bonita and the nearby post. Thomas himself had been a guest of Hooker's, from whom he heard a number of authentic accounts about the Territory in the early days. These the dramatist incorporated into his play, making them part of the lines written for a character patterned after Hooker himself. Thus the drama was a source of valid local history as well as an artistic production.[16]

Henry C. Hooker died in December of 1907, just a few days short of his eightieth birthday. His great house passed to his heirs, and his descendants still own it, living there and ranching a part of the vast spread Sierra Bonita cattle once ranged. In the course of years various alterations have been made to the house.[17] By the

The frame barn is an original structure.

The Sierra Bonita stables, focal point of a working ranch. The skylight is unique.

early 1880s, and before the Geronimo campaigns, the danger of Indian attack appeared over, and Hooker cut several windows and a central doorway into the house front, facing northeast.[18] The same wing was later deepened by enclosing a part of what once was the patio; this area now serves as a foyer and study and proudly contains Hooker's roll-top desk. A new lounge room was recently added to the northwest wing. The windmill and water tower no longer stand in the patio, and the well likewise is capped; in a secure age, courtyard space could be put to other use. The root cellar also has fallen into disuse, its entrance now being covered by flowers and trees. The removal of these once-essential facilities permitted the expansion of the house within, and the consequent reduction of the patio to an oblong forty by sixty feet.

When it was built, the Sierra Bonita ranch house offered luxury and refinement within the idiom of a traditional building form. The fact that it survives today largely unaltered, still serving as a home and headquarters for an important ranch, bears eloquent testimony to the soundness of its plan and construction and to the comfort which its proud but far-seeing owner demanded. No less than the older and smaller houses of Pete Kitchen and Emilio Carrillo, the Sierra Bonita provided an answer, at once practical and graceful, to the problems of Southwestern living.

The Triumph of Expansion

*The Empire complex from the courtyard, looking southwest. This unusual
photograph was made before the turn of the century.*

Empire

For years the Empire Ranch of southern Arizona grew by the addition of smaller adjacent properties to its vast spread, until at last it sprawled into three counties.[1] The house which served as headquarters for the Empire grew in the same way. Among the dwellings of ranchers in territorial Arizona, it represented the high point of accretion, or expansion by addition to an existing structure. From its beginning as a massive adobe house with four rooms and a large, imposing central hallway, the Empire's headquarters grew to a sprawling mansion of twenty-two rooms.[2] This growth reflected not merely the need for additional space but the importance of the ranch and the increasing prosperity of its owners.

The Empire Ranch was acquired about 1870 by Edward Nye Fish, a prominent Tucson merchant, in the name of his brother-in-law, William Wakefield. A later tradition maintained that Fish acquired the property — then consisting of 160 acres of land, together with horses and cattle — from a nameless Mexican, and that he paid the sum of $3,000 for it.[3] Whatever the truth of the story, Fish gave the ranch its name, and when he put it up for sale in July of 1876, the property included the large adobe dwelling that formed the nucleus for the great house which would rise there.

The merchant's asking price was $3,800, a sum he justified on the grounds that the improvements he had made on the property were worth more than a quarter of the total amount.[4]

Fish's buyers were Walter L. Vail and Herbert R. Hislop, two young men of means. Vail had decided during his New Jersey childhood that he would find his destiny in the West.[5] By 1875 he had left his home and migrated to Virginia City, Nevada, where he worked as a timekeeper in a mine. Learning at first hand the hazards of mining and the uncertainties of many a promising strike, he soon decided to seek another field for his talents and capital. In the autumn of that year he traveled to California and probably there consulted his uncle, Nathan Vail, about the possibility of obtaining backing in a ranching venture. Evidently the older Vail's answer was affirmative, for in November the young man went to Arizona and there surveyed the prospects for establishing himself as a stockman.[6] His reactions were mixed. "I feel positive from all I hear," he wrote to his younger brother in the East, "that there is as fine grass land in this territory as there is in the *world*."[7] On the other hand, Indian difficulties, and the fact that Anglo-American occupation of the area was so recent, made the acquisition of land titles very difficult. He could settle on his homestead (160 acres) and pre-empt more by controlling the water courses, but there would be no security to his claim. The only way to be sure of ownership was to purchase land from someone who had already held it for three years. On balance, the outlook in Arizona seemed unfavorable to the young man: ". . . gambling, Indians and drinking is the ruination of the country," he concluded. Although it might be possible to make money once the railroad had penetrated the Territory and the Indians had been subdued, he would not recommend that any Easterner come out right away.[8]

Evidently Walter Vail soon reversed this judgment. While he returned to work in Nevada, his uncle Nathan sought backers for the ranching venture. By the following April, the older man had found three potential partners for his nephew. One of these, Herbert Hislop, was a young Englishman from a wealthy and influential family whom Vail had met when in London assisting in the installation of that city's first street-car system.[9] Like many another of his countrymen, Hislop was dazzled by glowing reports of the wealth to be made from cattle ranching in the American West and eagerly sought the opportunity to cast his lot and means with such a dramatic future. Gladly accepting Nathan Vail's proposition, he set sail for the United States in May of 1876 and late the following month met Walter Vail in San Francisco. From there the two young men started the slow trip to Arizona, where they arrived, after a gruelling journey by boat, train, and stage, in mid-July. Stopping at Florence en route to Tucson, they learned from newspapers that Fish had placed his ranch on the market. Vail had seen the property the previous year, and had admired it. He understood, however, that the ranch was stocked with more cattle than it had carried previously, and for that reason doubted whether he and Hislop would be able to meet the purchase price.[10]

Vail was too pessimistic. Though the young partners looked at a number of ranches near Tucson, they settled, before the end of August, on the Empire spread.[11] Located some forty-five miles southeast of the town, it was ringed on three sides with mountains, while to the south it dominated a long, wide, and rolling valley which descended from the Huachuca range. The well-watered country was blanketed by tall range grass and reminded Hislop of the South Downs in his native England. The house, he noted, was "nicely situated" at the top of a rise; behind it were a sturdy adobe corral, a stable, and a well which Fish had fenced, presum-

*Key men of the
English Boys' Outfit—
John Harvey, Edward
Vail and Walter Vail,
1879.*

The original headquarters on the Empire, built before Vail bought the property in 1876.

ably to prevent contamination of the water supply. Beyond there extended a fenced field enclosing twenty acres, and at one corner a small, separate house.[12]

In a letter to Nathan Vail, Hislop noted that the main ranch house "might be made very comfortable indeed with laying out a little money on it." Of the four rooms, each twenty feet square, the front two were designed for sleeping purposes, while the two behind served respectively for storage and as a kitchen. The dominant feature of the dwelling was the central hallway, eighteen feet wide by forty long, which divided it into two equal wings and gave upon a large corral one hundred feet square, designed to hold cattle secure from Apache attack.[13] The roof of the structure was peaked, but it was made of mud and, Hislop observed, leaked badly during periods of heavy rain. Within the house all the floors also were mud, so the drainage did little harm beyond the discomfort it caused the inhabitants. Windows and doors were empty openings, devoid of shutters, glass, or even canvas to repel the fury of seasonal storms. The dwelling contained no furniture. Hislop wrote of his first visit in July of 1876 that he "went to bed which consisted of lying on the mud floor with a blanket round you and no windows in the house, but for all that I slept like a top."[14]

For the first months of their occupancy, Hislop and Vail led a Spartan existence. Their unvarying fare was meat and bread, a diet which became insufferably monotonous as the months passed, notwithstanding Hislop's best efforts as cook to vary it with such delicacies as a homemade plum pudding at Christmas. As to the house, the life it afforded was primitive. In their bedroom, the Englishman wrote, he and Vail had lizards and bats — "but we do not mind these," he hastily added; "they are harmless." Nevertheless, the partners soon set to work to make the dwelling more habitable. Within a month after they bought the ranch, they had hired two Indians to plaster inner walls and had gone to Tucson to recruit other labor, as "we intend to live as comfortable as this country will let us." But the tasks of carpentry they reserved to themselves; in Tucson a carpenter's wages were five dollars a day, Hislop reported, so he and Vail made all the windows and doors for the

The central hallway, eighteen feet wide by forty feet long.

house, and did other necessary wood work.[15] Soon they built or bought rudimentary furniture: bedsteads, mattresses, tables, and chairs. Hislop even procured a large tin tub in Tucson. Although he complained to his sister in England about the ten dollars it cost him, this convenience allowed him to bathe — in cold water — every morning. Still, one economy remained particularly irksome. With lumber costing twelve to fourteen cents per board foot delivered at the ranch, the partners could not afford to lay floors in the house. "How I should appreciate a carpet or bare boards," the Englishman exclaimed after nine months at the Empire. Dirt floors, though cheap, were "rather miserable and awfully dirty."[16]

Such frontier discomforts failed to daunt the young men. Very soon after taking over the Empire Ranch, they began to demonstrate the business acumen and farsightedness which would make it great. As early as September of 1876, they had bought a sheep ranch which adjoined their spread; they had no use for the sheep, save for meat and as articles of barter, but they knew that they had to expand their holdings.[17] "At present," Hislop wrote that month, "we must do all in our power to get all the land we can as I easily see a stock ranch cannot be carried on in a limited space, but needs any amount of land . . . it is not a country for a poor man."[18] Within five years the Empire Ranch had absorbed the nearby Sanford, Kane, and Gardiner spreads. It continued to grow until its holdings covered a region of a thousand square miles, reaching from the Rincon Mountains to the Mexican border, and spanning the country between the Santa Cruz and San Pedro rivers.[19]

As the Empire Ranch grew, so did its herd. As early as October, 1876, Hislop facetiously remarked that theirs was "the best ranch in the territory," needing "only . . . about 5000 head of cattle on it to make it complete." By the next spring they had about eight hundred cows and many calves, and Walter Vail went to New

49

An adobe barn closes one side of the headquarters courtyard.

50

Mexico to purchase forty head of blooded Durham bulls to improve the stock line. Within three years, further purchases and natural increase had brought the herd to over five thousand animals, and the ranch was well on its way to becoming one of the most important cattle outfits in Arizona Territory.[20]

Walter Vail had a succession of partners in the Empire venture. Before the end of 1876 he and Hislop were joined by another young Englishman, John N. Harvey; Arizonans promptly dubbed the ranch the "English Boys' Outfit." Less than two years later Hislop was forced to return to England because of a crisis in his financial affairs; though he came back to the United States and spent the rest of a long life there, he had nothing more to do with the Empire. In 1879 Vail's younger brother, Edward, came west from New York to learn the cattle business. Though the greenhorn did not buy into the Empire Ranch, Walter consolidated his ownership by buying out Harvey. Apparently the price was good. The Englishman went to New York, where he lived in the lavish style befitting a cattle baron, but according to a tradition in the Vail family, he died working as an ordinary laborer in a California mine.[21] In the 1880s Vail took on Carrol V. Gates as a partner, but apparently the association lasted less than a decade. At all times from 1879 until his death in 1906, Walter Vail retained principal ownership of the ranch.

Like many other men of means, Vail diversified his holdings. One opportunity to do so came about 1883 when, with Gates, he purchased the Total Wreck mining claims in the Empire Mountains for the back taxes which had accumulated. The site was covered with so many quartz boulders that the discoverer described it as a "total wreck." The name stuck. Nathan Vail came from California to help manage the mine and a thriving camp grew up near the site. By the time Walter Vail sold the property to a New

York corporation, it had produced half a million ounces of silver.[22]

From the time he acquired the Empire, Walter added to the ranch house as more space was required. In the autumn of 1876, when the partners had only two ranch hands, the hired men slept in the storage room of the original adobe and ate with their employers. Within the next five years, the house grew by five rooms as a kitchen, office, cook's room, pantry, and other facilities were needed. Perhaps at this time too the frame house already mentioned went up nearby to accommodate the growing work force of cowboys employed on the ranch. [23]

In 1884 the biggest expansion occurred. In that year Walter Vail returned to New Jersey for a visit and there married a young wife. When the couple came back to Arizona, Vail built his bride a sumptuous house, attached to the additions he had already made to the original dwelling.[24] The walls of this new building were twenty inches thick, and its ceilings nearly twelve feet high. The front door opened off a covered porch into a living room fifteen feet long, warmed in winter by fires in a great stone fireplace. The outstanding feature of this room was its half-hexagon bay window,[25] a highly popular element of Gothic Revival architecture in the East and a decided novelty in the Arizona countryside where glass was still something of a rarity. Adjoining the living room to the west was the dining room, which shared a common wall with the older construction. The two most southerly rooms of the enlarged original house now were converted to use as a pantry and kitchen respectively. Completing the 1884 house were two large bedrooms, heated by a double fireplace of the same construction as the one in the living room. The entire addition was surmounted by an imposing gable roof of riven shake shingles.

Even at this point the house was not yet complete. Later construction added two more bedrooms to the south, continuing the

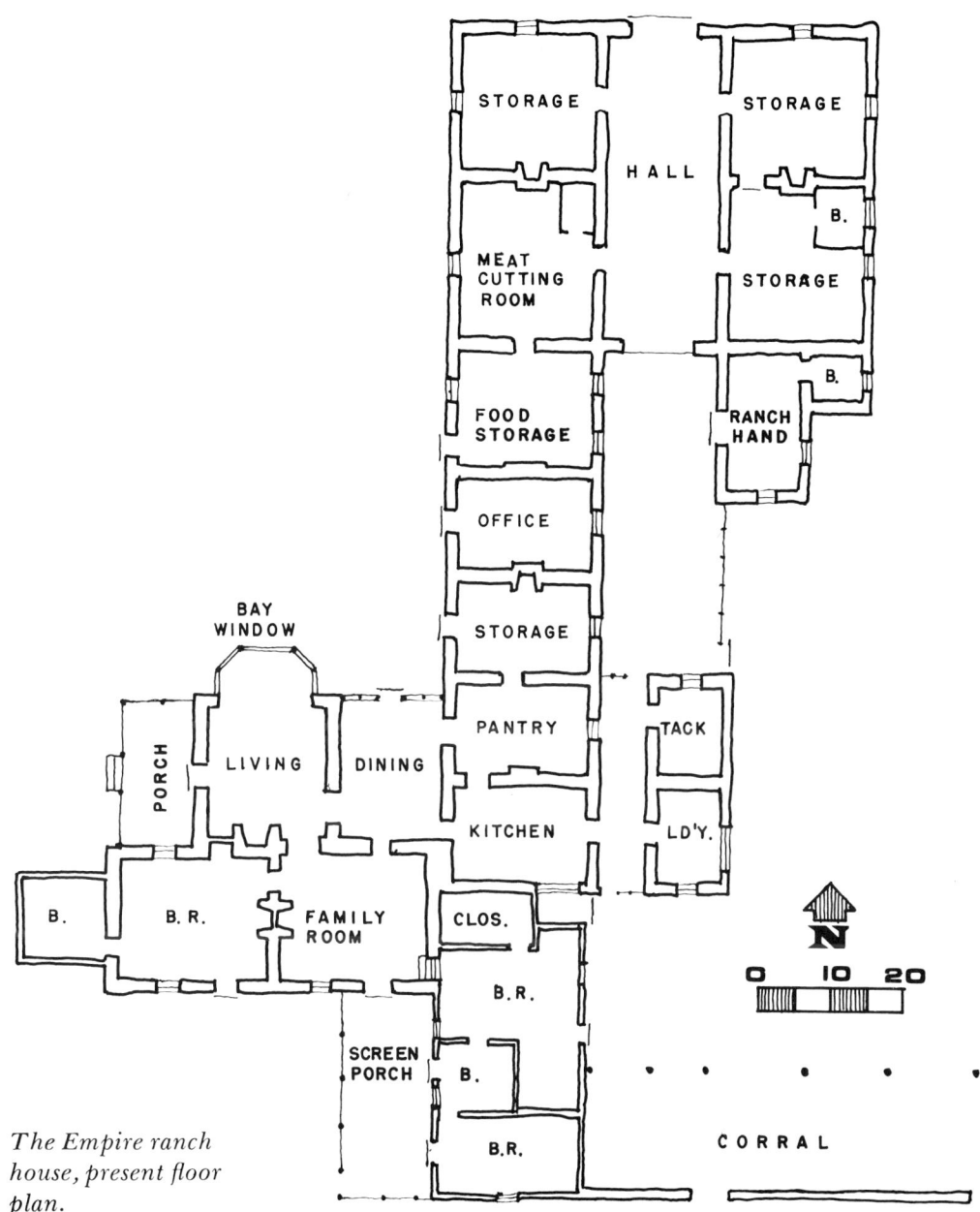

STORAGE STORAGE

HALL

MEAT
CUTTING
ROOM

STORAGE

B.

FOOD
STORAGE

RANCH
HAND

OFFICE

STORAGE

BAY
WINDOW

PANTRY

TACK

PORCH

LIVING DINING

LD'Y.

KITCHEN

N

0 10 20

B. B.R.

FAMILY
ROOM

CLOS.

B.R.

SCREEN
PORCH

B.

CORRAL

*The Empire ranch
house, present floor
plan.*

B.R.

The Vail house as it appears today. An outstanding feature is the half-hexagon bay window.

long wing of additions to the original dwelling. Screened porches, baths, service rooms, and a sleeping room for ranch hands completed the structure at last.

Walter Vail, his wife, and their growing family left the Empire Ranch in 1896 for Los Angeles. The Vails already owned property in southern California including Catalina Island, which they used for pasture land on which to fatten up cattle on the way to market.[26] Retaining the Empire, Vail expanded his holdings on the coast, culminating his career in 1904–05 by forming a giant ranch of 103,000 acres from land embraced in four Mexican land grants in Riverside County. After his death in 1906, his son Mahlon moved back to Arizona and assumed management of the Empire; another son, William Banning Vail, took charge of the property in 1913. Other heirs managed the rest of the family's large holdings.[27]

In 1928 the Vail family sold the Empire to Henry, Frank and Charles Boice, owners of the Chiricahua Cattle Company and proprietors of several other spreads in southern Arizona. For nearly forty years more the great cattle ranch continued to operate under Boice management. Then in 1960 the property changed hands again. The Gulf American Corporation acquired it, intending to develop it as a satellite city to Tucson. The director and staff of the Arizona Historical Society, however, became concerned about preserving the ranch house as a monument to one of Arizona's pioneer ranching families and as a splendid relic of a bygone era. As a result, the corporation donated the building to the Society for a museum in which the history of Arizona's cattle industry would be graphically interpreted. Those who visit the museum will see in its original state an excellent illustration of pure Mexican building tradition joined compatibly with a nineteenth-century Victorian eclectic house.

The headquarters at Faraway, virtually unchanged since its completion about 1890.

New Styles

Faraway

San Bernardino

BY THE MID-1880s the influence of the railroad had made itself felt on domestic architecture in the most remote parts of southern Arizona. The result of access to the ideas, styles, and materials of other sections of the country soon became apparent. Although builders continued, of necessity, to use native materials for exterior wall construction, they departed radically from the Spanish-Mexican adobe idiom in other ways. The process of divorce from the native vernacular was progressive, however, and the evolution of a decisively Anglo-American architectural style and building technique, though rapid, did not occur instantaneously. Two structures built in southern Arizona during 1888 and 1889, the Faraway and San Bernardino ranch houses, illustrated the changing trend in taste. In so doing, they also demonstrated the increasing breakdown of regional style before the assault of ideas from a wider world.

With his bride of a year, Neil Erickson, the son of a Swedish immigrant, homesteaded the Faraway Ranch in 1888. The land he claimed lay near Dos Cabezas, southeast of Willcox, in upper Cochise County, a region rapidly becoming known as one of the best ranch areas in Arizona.[1] Formerly first sergeant of a cavalry troop, Erickson had been stationed at Forts Huachuca and Bowie,

The Faraway house, in the shadow of the rugged Chiricahua Mountains, from the southeast.

and knew the area well. Possibly he had even been detailed to duty
for a time on Faraway land; family tradition maintains that the
small adobe and stone house on his property had served as headquarters for a temporary army encampment. Whatever the truth
of the story, the building had fallen into bad disrepair by the time
Erickson took up the land, and in the winter of 1888–1889 he de-
molished two of its three rooms, preserving only one to serve as
shelter during the time he was constructing his house.[2] Behind this
single room he dug a well to provide an adequate water supply,
using the soil from this excavation to reinforce the upper parts of
the old walls and raise them to a height of nine feet. He then laid
stones on the face of the original adobe to increase wall depth to
twenty-eight inches. With the existing structure thus strengthened,
he proceeded to build onto it until it became the nucleus for an
imposing and handsome house.[3]

First Erickson added a kitchen and living-dining room, built
of adobe, to the west and south of the original room which thence-
forth served as cold storage for perishable goods, the original
entrance becoming the present doorway into the adjoining kitchen.
Next, three bedrooms and a storage area were added above, to
complete a second story. The floors of these additions were of
four-inch pine planks, their construction a significant reflection
of improvements in transportation over the preceding decade.
Access to the upper story was gained by a steep and narrow enclosed
stairway which rose from the living-dining room and completed a
full circle before reaching the second floor. Above the upper story
was a partially floored attic which afforded still more room for
storage. Three dormer windows, projecting out from a massive
shingled hipped roof, ventilated this area.[4]

Numerous innovations in style at the Faraway ranch house
marked significant departures from the native regional tradition.

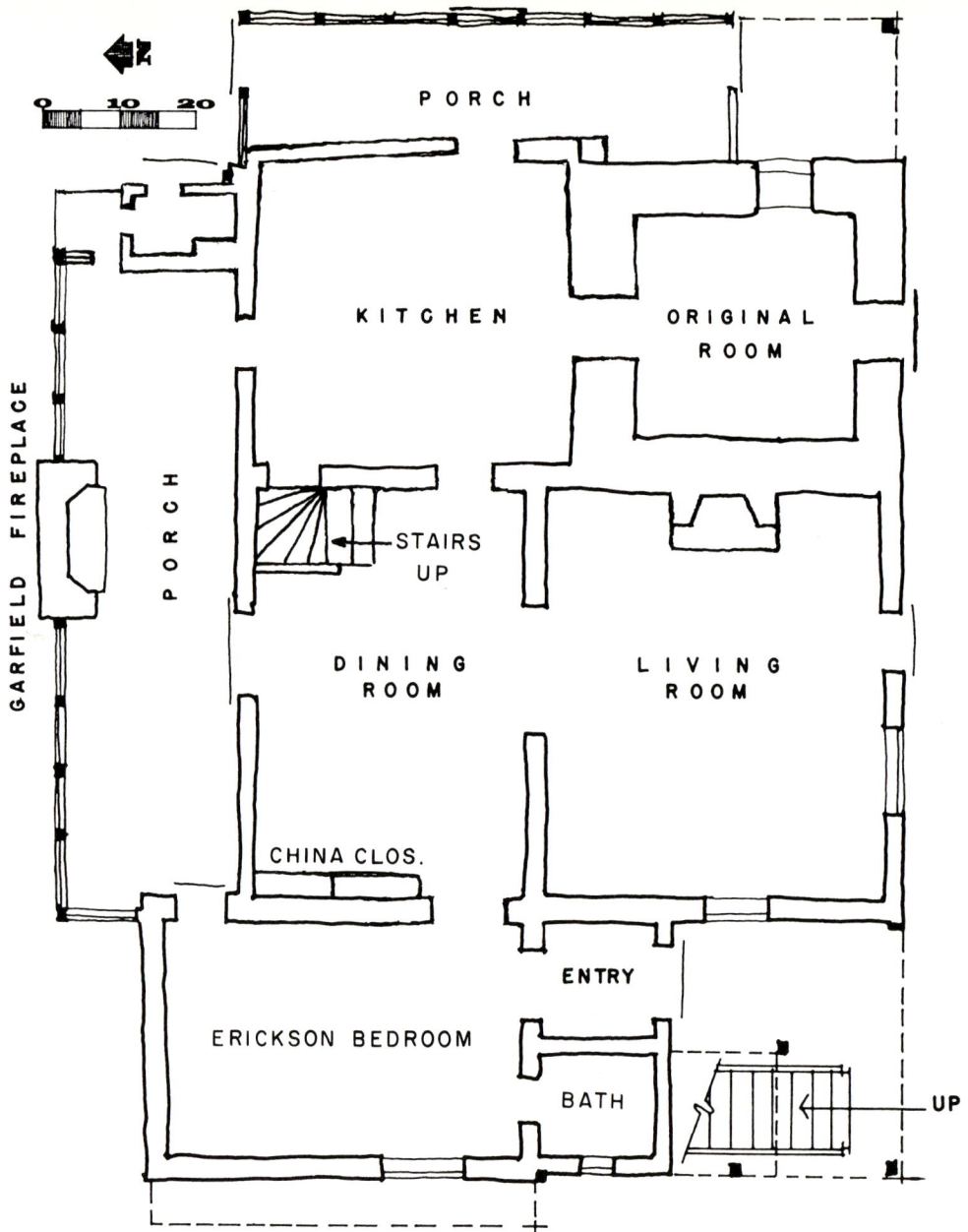

The Faraway ranch house, present floor plan.

The dining room, showing Erickson's skill as a carpenter.

First and most important, it was the first country house in southern Arizona to have more than a single story. Within, Erickson's skill as a carpenter and craftsman and the influence of Eastern copy books and building manuals were apparent in many details. Since dimensioned lumber was now available, wooden door jambs, window sashes, and sills were crafted in a fashion reminiscent of Eastern dwellings. Wooden cabinet work enhanced the appearance of the dining room, also recalling the styles of the eastern seaboard. Indeed, the entire dwelling was suggestive of the "growing houses" of colonial New England, which expanded from one- or two-room dwellings, developing according to the needs of their inhabitants. Here, however, the additions were contained within a closed geometric form rather than spreading, as New England houses did, by the addition of ells and wings.[5]

Neil Erickson's painstaking craftsmanship plainly showed that he built his house to last. Nevertheless, before the end of his long

The Garfield fireplace.

life, he found it necessary to undertake extensive remodeling. In 1924 he added a glassed-in porch on the ground floor to the west of the house and a large bedroom, with porch and bath, to the south. At the same time, he expanded the living-room area on the east and built an outside staircase mounting to an interesting balustraded second-story balcony. The east upstairs bedroom was enlarged to complete the vertical line of the additions below. During this remodeling, interior plumbing also was installed on the ground floor of the house, and an imposing fireplace, made from the stones of an old army monument on the property, was erected on the new west porch, making it serviceable for year-round dining and other uses.

This "Garfield fireplace" was so called because after the assassination of President Garfield in 1881, the soldiers then encamped at that place erected a monument of stones three feet square and three feet high in his honor, inscribing on it the name or initials of each man in the company. Since it was in poor condition at the time of the 1924 renovation, it was incorporated into the fireplace on the enclosed porch. There it rendered good service, for then as now the house had no central heating.

The Faraway ranch house stands as an interesting midpoint between two architectural traditions. Properly neither Spanish-Mexican nor nineteenth-century American, it contained elements of both. Since Erickson had sought to imitate neither style, his dwelling was, above all, personal and individual, a charming blend of two heritages. It remains comfortable and serviceable to the present day, still in the hands of Erickson's descendants, and still the headquarters of a seven-thousand-acre ranch. The Faraway house is a particularly pleasant architectural bridge over eighty-five years of Arizona's history.

The San Bernardino complex, 1887.

San Bernardino

With the building of John Horton Slaughter's San Bernardino ranch house in 1887–1888, territorial ranch architecture for the first time showed a decisively Anglo-American character. As was the case at Faraway, the primary building material remained adobe, but Slaughter's house had as little in common with Erickson's as with the contiguous-room frontier fortresses built two decades earlier, or the *hacienda* houses which represented the highest articulation of the Spanish-Mexican architectural idiom. Since the San Bernardino house was built all at one time, its construction departed from the native builder's additive tradition as well. Indeed, with its massive roof, broad verandas, and sense of interior spaciousness, it represented a different style altogether, recalling the Southern background of Slaughter himself, a native of Louisiana who had grown up in south Texas.[6]

The San Bernardino Ranch occupied the greater part of an important Mexican land grant, made in 1822 to Lieutenant Ignacio

Pérez. Its lands originally spanned both sides of the present international line, encompassing nearly 75,000 acres in southeastern Arizona and northeastern Sonora.[7] Prior to 1835, Pérez stocked his ranges with 100,000 head of cattle. His home and ranch headquarters, covering between two and three acres, occupied the site of a Spanish presidio which functioned between 1775 and 1780.[8] By the mid-1830s Apache hostilities through much of upper Sonora had grown so intense that the frontier of settlement had to retreat southward and the San Bernardino was abandoned, together with its huge cattle herd. The ranch house soon fell into decay.[9] Anglo argonauts following the southern trail to the gold fields in the late 1840s occasionally mentioned its spacious ruins, and United States Boundary Commissioner John Russell Bartlett left a detailed description of what still stood on the site in 1851.[10] The most prominent ruin was of a building about one hundred feet square, with a spacious courtyard at its center. The entire ranch complex was surrounded by an adobe wall whose defensive bastions were still visible.[11]

Throughout Arizona's early territorial period, the grazing lands of the San Bernardino lay idle, since the property remained in Mexican hands. With the discovery of silver at Tombstone in 1877, however, a mining boom began, and beef to feed the miners soon was at a premium.[12] A cowman from early in his life, Slaughter was attracted by the country and the prospect alike.[13] After ranching in various parts of southern Arizona, he bought 65,000 acres of the San Bernardino grant from its owner, G. Andrade of Guaymas, in 1886. Shortly afterwards he erected a small adobe house, with adjoining stables and other outbuildings, near the site of the old *hacienda*. The following year, however, a great earthquake in northern Sonora devastated much of the region and completely destroyed Slaughter's modest dwelling.[14] Undaunted, the rancher

65

The house and dependencies as they look today.

The main house from the southwest.

soon commenced construction of a much larger and finer house and dependencies.[15]

John Slaughter built his great home atop a rise which commanded a long, grassy valley below. A massive hipped roof, covered with imported cedar shingles, completely dominated the structure. A long porch ran the length of the south side and was extended to provide shade on the east and west sides. This porch was supported by millwork posts with square bases and capitals. These were common at the turn of the century and could have been ordered from any mail-order catalog. Above, under the gable, a large attic provided storage room for many household goods. Below, the front door faced west, opening into a through-hall five feet wide which separated the two wings of the house. Of these, the northern one was the longer. It ended in a large kitchen, where cooking for the whole ranch was done, and in an adjoining area which served at first as a dining room for Mexican and black ranch hands but

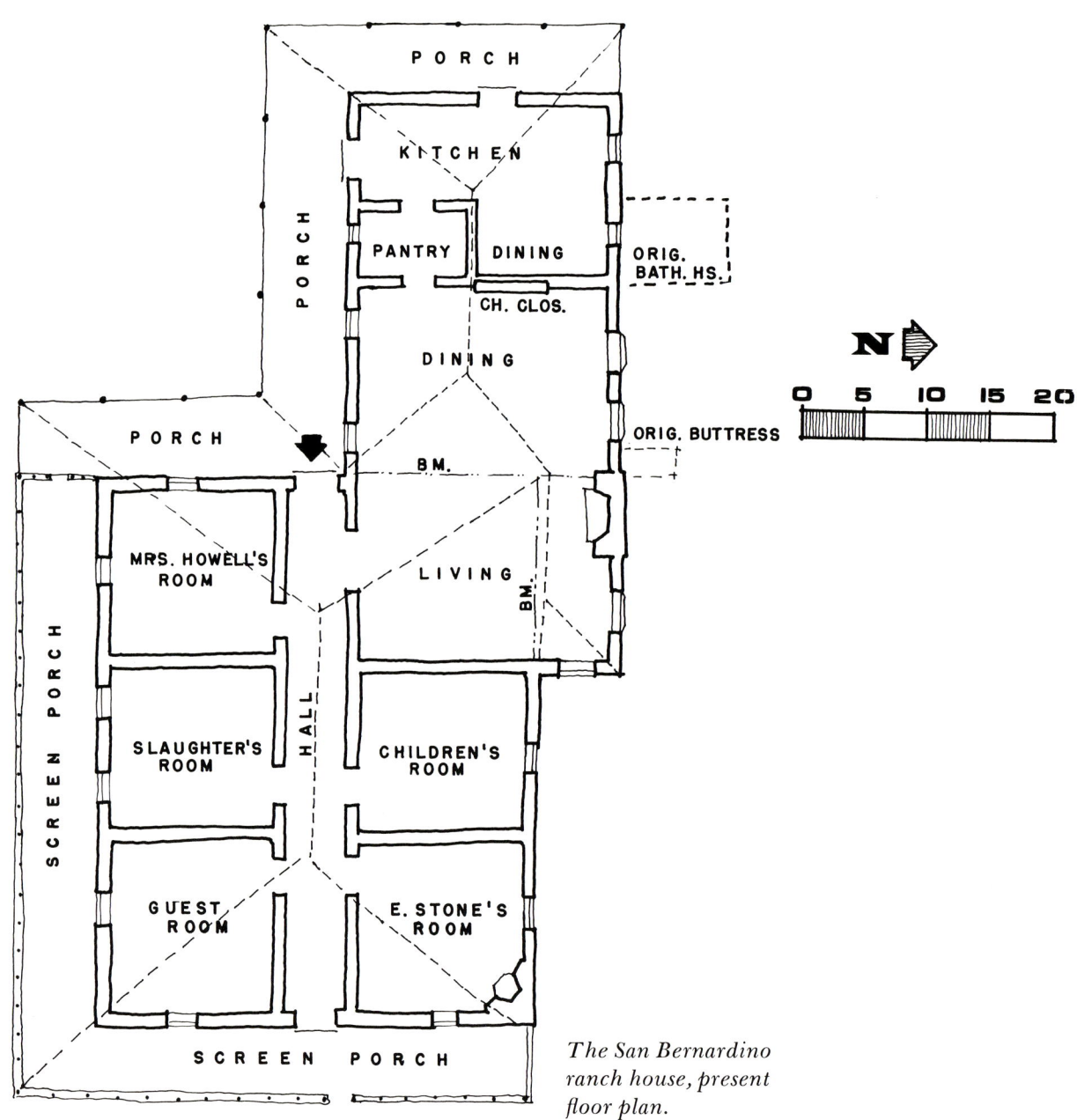

PORCH

KITCHEN

PORCH

PANTRY DINING

ORIG. BATH. HS.

CH. CLOS.

DINING

N

0   5   10   15   20

PORCH

ORIG. BUTTRESS

BM.

MRS. HOWELL'S ROOM

LIVING

BM.

SCREEN PORCH

HALL

SLAUGHTER'S ROOM

CHILDREN'S ROOM

GUEST ROOM

E. STONE'S ROOM

SCREEN PORCH

The San Bernardino ranch house, present floor plan.

later was adapted for use as a pantry. To the east, the kitchen opened into a spacious chamber which served as both living and dining room for Slaughter, his family, and the many guests who visited the ranch. This room was the center of social and family life, especially in the evenings, when the large dining-room table held one of the two lamps in the house. It was there that Slaughter entertained such guests as Emilio Kosterlitzky of the Mexican *rurales* and Generals George Crook and Nelson A. Miles of the United States forces. The Slaughters liked to socialize and kept open house at the ranch.

East of the living-dining room were two good-sized bedrooms; the south wing included three more. All measured about twelve feet by twelve, although none was perfectly square. Only one, in the northeast corner, had a fireplace — the room of Slaughter's secretary. The rancher, his wife, and his children slept in unheated rooms.[16]

The San Bernardino ranch house embodied a number of architectural innovations suggestive of the relative ease and security of frontier living at the time it was built. Slaughter never had any trouble with the Apaches. Like Colonel Hooker of the Sierra Bonita he let them have a few head of cattle from time to time to be free of depredation, and since he showed no fear of leaders like Geronimo, they respected him. There was less to fear, of course, when the Apache wars ended at last in 1886, and although bandits remained a problem in the border country, the absence of Indian danger made it possible to build a house much more open and airy than earlier dwellings had been. Every room except the pantry had exterior fenestration, and there were three outer doors. Windows in the living-dining room were large — six feet high — and began only nine inches above the floor. The width of the spacious hall separating the two parts of the house suggests that it may have

*Innovations and refinements in Slaughter's house suggest the relative
ease and security of its period. The china cabinet was a mail-order luxury,
shipped by rail from the East.*

been designed to serve as a social area, supplementing the living room; weight is lent to this conjecture by the fact that one of the two lamps in the house was in the hall.[17]

Improved transportation contributed directly to the elegance and comfort of the San Bernardino ranch house. Like Faraway, it had pine flooring in every room. Unlike Erickson's house, it contained ornamental features in the very height of late-nineteenth-century taste. Soon after building his dwelling, Slaughter procured a china cabinet, which was set into the kitchen wall next to the pantry. At the same time he also got a diamond-pane window with a classical cornice frame; this he set into the wall of the living-dining room. Both of these embodiments of revivalism probably were mail order purchases, shipped by rail to Arizona from cities in the East or Midwest. To complete these embellishments, a bathing room with running water was erected outside the kitchen. This facility remained in use until after the turn of the century, when Slaughter had plumbing installed inside the house.[18]

Behind the main house stood structures vital to the functioning of the ranch. On the west side was a small natural-stone building where vegetables, meat, and cheeses were stored. Beside it, another stone structure served as a commissary and general store, where ranch hands and their families could buy the necessities of life. Next to the store stood an adobe bunkhouse for the Mexican hands, and quarters for a Chinese cook.[19] Nearby there was a schoolhouse where Slaughter's two children received the rudiments of education together with the offspring of other ranch families and the numerous homeless waifs — black, white, and Indian — whom Slaughter and his wife sheltered and cared for.[20] This building was constructed on the "dog-run" or "possum-trot" plan, having two parallel sections, each with its own chimney, and a breezeway between, the entire structure covered by a single roof. This house

The living room in 1973. Slaughter installed the diamond-pane window.

style was widely used in the South, and Slaughter became familiar with it in Louisiana and Texas.[21] His house in Texas was built in this style. Beyond this collection of dependencies stood other buildings — barns and granaries, workshops, a blacksmith's shop, and even a post office. The ranch included 600 acres of farm land, watered by ten artesian wells, which produced wheat, barley, corn, fruits and vegetables. With such an aggregation of structures and productive activities, the San Bernardino became virtually a self-contained, autonomous community.

Notwithstanding the luxuries of Slaughter's great house, life at the San Bernardino was probably more Spartan than it was on other large Arizona cattle ranches in the late 1880s and 1890s.[22] Some of the simplicity perhaps was attributable to the character of its owner. Though hospitable and genial, Slaughter had a flintiness about him which suggested a thoroughly businesslike approach to the problems of living. His determination served him well as a rancher, and no less so as the three-term sheriff of Cochise County who cleaned up Tombstone in the late eighties.[23] For this man there was little leisure and less self-indulgence, and life on the San Bernardino Ranch took its lead from him. Everyone worked. Assisted by the cook and other women on the place, Mrs. Slaughter preserved the fruits and vegetables which grew in the large gardens her husband had cleared. In a kettle behind the kitchen she made the lye soap with which domestic servants scrubbed the pine floors of the big house. Slaughter himself was continually active around the ranch, supervising the work of his hired men and handling the complex details involved in managing such a large enterprise. Home life was similarly businesslike; two lamps sufficed in the house because most of its inhabitants went to bed with the sun. Food was plentiful but simple. There were three meals daily, beginning with breakfast right after sunrise and ending with an early supper, and beef was the staple at each.[24]

John Slaughter continued active as the proprietor of the San Bernardino Ranch until 1921, the year before his death, when he turned over control to his grandson, John Green, and retired to the town of Douglas, Arizona. Since his day, very few changes have been made in the house or its dependencies. The "possum-trot" schoolhouse has disappeared, as have some of the further outbuildings. North of the ranch house a large pond or stock tank gives an illusion of coolness rare in the desert Southwest. The house itself now has screened enclosures instead of open porches. It also has modern plumbing. Apart from these minor alterations, the compound of ranch buildings remains what it was when built more than three-quarters of a century ago. This integrity is a remarkable testimony to the practicality of its design, the quality of its workmanship, and its adaptability to the changing needs of a great ranch.

The Eastern Invasion

The third house at San Rafael, dating from 1892.

San Rafael

THE BUILDING OF Colin Cameron's San Rafael ranch house in 1900 completed the evolution of territorial ranch architecture in Arizona. Triumphant, the huge mansion stood atop a hill commanding the grasslands for miles around, a proud boast that the southwestern rancher had met and conquered the hazards of nature, Indians and outlaws.[1] Even as the victory belonged to the Anglo-American in Arizona, so the great house defiantly departed from the regional idiom, expressing the tastes of the newcomer whose tenacity and skill had transformed the Southwest in the space of half a century.[2] No part or detail of the structure bespoke the Spanish-American tradition in architecture. Instead, it recalled a style which had originated in the West Indies and came to fruition in the Carolinas and Louisiana as the French colonial style.[3] The design was cosmopolitan, no longer identified with any region, but it expressed Cameron's opulence and importance. At the same time it afforded him and his family comforts still rare on the frontier.[4]

Cameron belonged to a family which had produced many rich and important people — senators, cabinet members, bankers, railroad magnates. A gathering place for the family and a focus for family affairs was Donegal, a twenty-five-room Georgian mansion in Lancaster County, Pennsylvania, which provided Cameron with some of his ideas when he began building in Arizona and gave him a model on which to base his style of living.

Cameron's mansion was the fourth headquarters ranch house to rise at San Rafael. The earliest, a simple strip-form adobe, was in existence when he acquired the land in 1884, and he added to it as need dictated until it grew to the unprecedented size of seven contiguous rooms. A second house, standing near the site of the later mansion, was built in the early 1880s by some mining men; Cameron bought it for a fraction of its value, enlarged it to ten rooms, and lived in it until 1892, when he erected a larger and more elegant residence to house his wife and their growing family.[5]

This third house furnished confirmation of the adage that people carry their native architectural traditions with them, for, though built with adobe, it corresponded closely to the style of country building in Cameron's native Pennsylvania. Rectangular in plan and very large, the main portion of the house had two floors, while a single-story service wing was attached to a rear corner of the structure.[6] Around three sides, a broad porch with finished colonnettes extended, and brick chimneys with cornices and wood-trimmed sash windows were added refinements. Otherwise the lines were classical, with window above window or door, and the ends of the house pierced symmetrically. Within there were fifteen rooms, including four baths — a luxury unprecedented in Arizona, where the best most houses afforded was a "bathing room" without interior plumbing.[7]

This third San Rafael house burned mysteriously on Christmas Eve of the year 1899. More than a suggestion existed that the fire resulted from arson. The previous spring, a "Settlers Protective Association" had destroyed several of Cameron's fences, then warned that if he took legal action against any of the group's

76

The San Rafael ranch headquarters, built by Cameron in 1900, looking northwest.

members or tried to rebuild the fences, they would burn all his corrals and "every ranch you own or pretend to own" in the San Rafael Valley.[8] Cameron's house and part of its contents were destroyed in the fire; only a single chimney remained standing, later to become the nucleus of a hut for trappers. The rancher, however, was undaunted. He moved his family back into the older house that stood nearby, and there he soon was busy planning the great mansion he would build. It would be "the finest ranch house ever seen on a cattle ranch," commented the Phoenix *Arizona Republican* late in 1900, when construction was nearly complete.

> It is three stories high and contains thirty rooms. The house is equipped with modern conveniences, heated by acetylene gas, water is provided by storage tanks and carried throughout the house....

The newspaper story conveyed Cameron's intentions quite accurately. The fourth house at San Rafael was to be an imperial structure appropriate to the 600,000-acre ranch it commanded.[9]

The exterior of the house bore a strong resemblance to the ideal French colonial mansion of Parlange in Pointe Coupée Parish, Louisiana. This structure, built about 1750, was the prototype of what became known as the Southern Raised Cottage.[10] The style, somewhat modified, first appeared in the West in the home of Thomas O. Larkin, a merchant and later United States Consul in Monterey, California.[11] Larkin, who built his house in 1834, probably derived inspiration for it in North Carolina, where he had visited several times in the preceding decade.[12] There he had ample opportunity to observe the adaptability of the raised cottage to the moist climate of the coastal South which found some parallel in coastal California. By the end of the nineteenth century the style had been adopted by Victorian builders, who took it far from its original regions and used it for its elegance, irrespective of the dictates of climate. The raised cottage had made its appearance in Arizona, in fact, more than a decade before Cameron built his great house at San Rafael. Old Main, the original building on the campus of the University of Arizona, exemplified the style.[13]

Although the exterior of the San Rafael ranch house was imitative, Cameron and his wife varied the interior patterns sufficiently so the house reflected their personalities. Only the finest materials were used in construction. Brick for the outer walls was made from native clay but fired in kilns built on the property — a far cry from the customary adobe construction of the Southwest. Exterior doors and trim were of California redwood, which Cameron used because of its handsome color and its durability in intense heat.

The San Rafael house had three stories, including a full basement. The hipped roof, which dominated the whole structure, covered a wide veranda around the entire ground floor; the edge

The veranda.

The kitchen.

of the roof was supported by delicate colonnettes, squared at top and bottom. The veranda rested upon heavy brick pillars, raising it substantially above ground level and allowing light to the windows of the basement rooms. Above, the roof was pierced by six dormer windows and four rectangular chimneys with double cornices. Brick-arched windows embellished the exterior of the house, which was further ornamented by construction forms such as herringbone cross framing and post and beam joints.[14]

Like other ranch houses of the period, Cameron's mansion had a dual purpose. It served as headquarters for a very large working spread, which in itself had several different divisions, and it was at the same time a home for its owner and his family. The basement expressed the public function of the house. Entrance from the outside was at the east end, and gave upon a long hall. A living room, two bedrooms with fireplaces and adjoining closets, and a bath, provided accommodation for the two Chinese house servants.

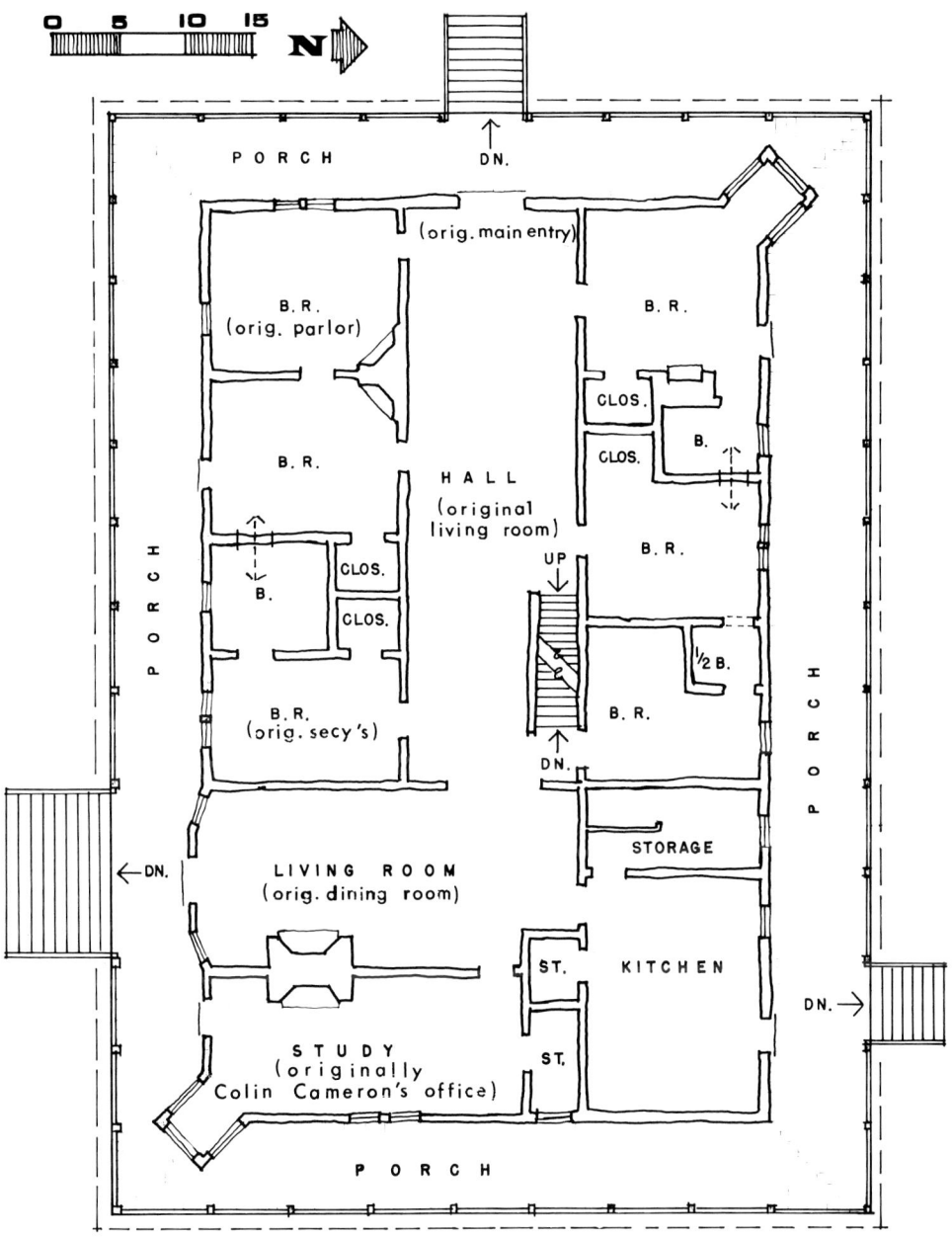

0 5 10 15

N

PORCH

DN.

(orig. main entry)

B.R.
(orig. parlor)

B.R.

CLOS.

CLOS.

B.

B.R.

PORCH

HALL
(original
living room)

B.R.

CLOS.

B.

CLOS.

UP

1/2 B.

B.R.

B.R.
(orig. secy's)

DN.

PORCH

DN.

LIVING ROOM
(orig. dining room)

STORAGE

STUDY
(originally
Colin Cameron's office)

ST.

KITCHEN

DN.

ST.

PORCH

The San Rafael ranch house, present arrangement of the main floor.

Several storerooms housed staple food supplies. Fruits and vegetables in season were stored in a cool-room. A dumb waiter transported foods to the kitchen on the floor above. Another basement area served as the ranch store, where hired hands received supplies. Coal and wood for the house fires were also stored below, and a reservoir for drinking water stood in the center of the long basement hallway. Rooms on this level were nicely finished with plastered walls and cement floors. Ceilings rose just four feet above the ground and windows were therefore high up in the walls.

Three outside staircases ascended to the veranda outside the main floor of the house. One led to the front door on the west, which in turn opened into a huge entry hall-living room. A second stair mounted to the door of Cameron's office on the south side of the house; thus employees could transact ranch business without passing through the family living areas. A third staircase provided outside access to the kitchen, situated in the northeast corner of the house. In addition to the ranch office and the kitchen, the main floor contained five bedrooms opening on the great hall, three baths, a parlor, a dining room and Cameron's private study, in addition to storage areas flanking the kitchen.[15]

The top floor of the house contained four bedrooms, two large and two small, and a bath. Dormer windows and a large hall skylight provided illumination and a sense of airy spaciousness to these rooms. Adjoining the bedrooms, ample storage areas occupied the corner spaces left by the overhanging roof.

Family living at San Rafael centered in the long center-hall living room, which stretched more than half the length of the house and ended at the door of the ranch office. With walls ten feet high, this spacious hall dominated the main floor of the dwelling. Cameron probably derived the idea for the room from the architecture of houses in rural Pennsylvania where through-halls

The great hall.

had been associated with the Georgian style of the eighteenth century. Although it lacked any outside openings apart from the front door, the hall was well lighted during the day by long windows in adjoining rooms, and at night by coal-oil lamps which shed a cheerful golden light. It was comfortably furnished and the walls were lined with bookcases.

In the southwestern corner of the house was the family parlor, a warm, pleasant room with red-leather chairs and walls painted yellow which were hung with prints and paintings. Here a piano provided many an evening of music, while numerous photographs of the prize cattle and horses Cameron had raised on his ranch gave testimony to his success as a pioneer stock breeder.

Luxury and elegance were the keynotes to life at Cameron's San Rafael home. Floors throughout the upper two stories, laid with native pine plank, were covered with English Wilton carpets or fine Navajo rugs. The furniture in the family quarters was Eastern and very good; some pieces were heirlooms which had passed down in Mrs. Cameron's family. All but two of the bedrooms were large enough to be furnished with double beds, bookcases, desks, and chairs, as well as the necessary chests of drawers; all were heated by either fireplaces or oil burners. Table linens, purchased in Philadelphia during frequent trips to the East, were imported from Europe, and Mrs. Cameron used fine sterling, crystal, and china.[16]

Just below the great house Cameron built a massive barn, in which rows of stalls housed his pure-bred saddle stock and the shetland ponies which he made a hobby of raising. The barn also furnished space for the manufacture of harness and other leather goods, and for a blacksmith's shop. Adjoining the barn, and at right angles to it, stood a machine shop; farther away there were five other service dependencies. Two enclosed pastures, each with

Colin Cameron, rancher and builder.

springs, served to segregate the best blooded Hereford cattle from the regular range stock, thereby assuring the success of Cameron's breeding program. Near the house were rose gardens and large orchards of fruit trees, while vegetables and melons grew in the so-called "China Garden" by the Santa Cruz River. This plot of land derived its name from the fact that it was farmed by three Chinese squatters, whom Cameron supplied with materials to build a shack and with seeds to plant. The rancher became the best customer for these enterprising newcomers, but other tenants on the San Rafael ranch also bought fresh produce there. According to family tradition, even those who could not afford to buy from the Chinese received food from the farm, Cameron quietly paying the bill.

In 1909, at the age of sixty, Colin Cameron sold the vast San Rafael ranch and its great house to William C. Greene, the Cananea copper magnate.[17] At this point the house ceased to be a family residence and became simply a ranch headquarters building. Greene levelled most of the outlying buildings, leaving only the barn and machine shop; such ancillary activities as saddle and harness making and butchering were moved to the basement or the top floor. Ranch cowboys were also moved into the big house, where they found quarters in the basement, sharing the area with the weapons and tack stored there. As befitted its new function, the house now lost some of its appealing ornamentation: Greene removed the veranda from the north side, sheathed the roof on the south side with metal, and took the fine wainscoting and chair rails out of the central hall. Apart from these changes, however, the building retained most of its structural integrity. When Greene's daughter, Florence Sharp, inherited the property, the house again became a family home.[18]

San Rafael, the last of southern Arizona's territorial ranch houses, and the finest in plan and construction, completed an evolution of thirty-four years. Regional ranch-house architecture grew from two distinct cultural traditions and mirrored the changing conditions on the southwestern frontier. The earliest houses were fortresses in which living was relatively primitive, and where much comfort was sacrificed to the demands of defense. These buildings expressed a frontier architectural idiom — not the finely developed architecture which evolved in central Mexico, but a simpler, less refined, and wholly practical style reflecting a concern for the basic necessities of life. Construction was from native adobe and wood, the primary materials locally available. As frontier living became safer, houses tended to become more elaborate, reflecting the character and prestige of their owners rather than merely the need to survive. Building remained in the Spanish-Mexican tradition, however, until the coming of the railroad in 1880 ended the isolation of southern Arizona. From that time forward, Anglo-American influences made themselves increasingly felt on regional architecture as builders first varied the older forms, then departed from the traditional techniques of construction. By the end of the nineteenth century, the native traditions had passed from the scene, giving way to specifically American structures, independent of the regional idiom in character, plan, and building materials. The change symbolized the final Americanization of the far Southwest.

Big Adobes, Little Adobes and Modern Adaptations

An early view of La Osa. The house dates from 1889.

THE HOUSES DISCUSSED in earlier chapters of this book graphically illustrate the development of southern Arizona ranch architecture during the territorial period. Several other noteworthy residences demonstrate the success of ranchers in coming to grips with the arid southwestern environment and the replacement of their practical building styles by elaborate structures embodying the refinements and elegancies of other traditions.

Some of them were, for their day, imposing buildings. Denton Sanford's ranch house on Sonoita Creek in present-day Santa Cruz County, built about 1874, was a four-room adobe but it was a spacious dwelling and the addition of three auxiliary buildings made the establishment "the finest hacienda in the Southwest."[1]

Denton Gregory Sanford, a New York stater, came West some time before 1860, homesteaded in 1874 on Sonoita Creek six miles northeast of the old village of Calabasas, and began work on his house at once.[2] In shape it recalled the Pete Kitchen and Tanque Verde structures, for it was constructed as a contiguous-room, flat-fronted building with an ell projecting toward the rear. The feature which distinguished Sanford's dwelling from its contemporaries, however, was the broad *zaguán*, eight feet wide, cutting through the center room. It served as lounging room and kitchen with a dutch oven for cooking and a long table with side benches for eating.[3]

The far south room belonged to Bertha Sanford, Denton's daughter. It was sixteen by twenty feet and provided space for bedding down any female visitors who came to the ranch. Denton's room, seventeen by twenty feet, was the largest. It was distinguished by a fireplace at the east end opposite a huge dark-colored bed whose headboard "seemed almost to reach the ceiling." Although the floors were of packed dirt and remained so during the entire occupancy, the walls were stuccoed and the house was probably highlighted by more refinements than could be found in any ranch house during the seventies other than Hooker's Sierra Bonita.[4]

The form, scale, plan, adobe wall materials and wood trim fall within the regional building traditions of southern Arizona. Later builders, however, added a new roof and other details, changing the profile of the house and covering the original Mexican structure so that it appeared to follow Eastern concepts.

Unhappily only the ruins of the old house and its three service dependencies remain today to suggest the quality of the life which once existed there. Sanford lost most of the property to the successors of Don Leon Herreras, who acquired the land as a grant in 1825.[5] Sanford's daughter Bertha Miller in 1925 sold what remained to Lee Zinsmeister of Pennsylvania who built the Circle Z guest ranch across Sonoita Creek from the original complex.[6]

Rail X

Another great adobe house was begun in 1880 on the Rail X, not far from Sanford's home and headquarters. Originally it was

Rail X, probably built about 1883 by Pennsylvanian Rollin R. Richardson.

built in the shape of a rectangular block about fifty feet long by twenty-five deep. The structure comprised four large rooms, equally distributed along both sides of a long through-hall which connected porches at the front and rear doors.[7] Beneath the kitchen, on the west side, was a root cellar for food storage. The house was of exposed adobe and had a flat dirt roof supported by *vigas*.[8] Later remodeling added a pitched roof, two flanking wings extending eastward, and a stucco coat on the adobe. The position of exterior doors also was changed.[9] In 1928 Oscar Ashburn, then owner of the Rail X, sold the house and ranch to Henry Boice of the Chiricahua Cattle Company. Since that time, many changes have been made in the interior, but the exterior remains much as it was early in the twentieth century. The dwelling still serves as headquarters for a working cattle ranch.

La Osa. It grew from a one-room adobe and now serves as a guest ranch.

La Osa

The ranch house at La Osa, near the village of Sasabe in southernmost Pima County, dates from 1889.[10] This handsome, flat-fronted adobe structure continued the additive tradition of regional architecture, for it began with a single room. Acquiring this shelter, Colonel William Sturges of Chicago expanded it with flanking rooms to the east and west, then added another row behind, creating a block two rooms deep.[11] Later owners enlarged the house considerably, constructing additions in a loose courtyard plan.[12] The complex of buildings has served for over forty years as one of southern Arizona's best-known guest ranches.[13]

Rail X and La Osa are excellent examples of ranch houses which changed and grew with changing times. Both began as expressions of the Mexican idiom but developed into hybrids, reflecting the affluence and physical needs of successive owners.

Canelo

These spacious (for their times) adobes were no more common on the frontier than little adobes — tiny and primitive structures with almost no comforts. Many an early-day rancher, unable or unwilling to build on a grand scale, got along with a few rooms built in Mexican style which provided him with living quarters and served as the nerve center for a very large ranch enterprise. Three may be mentioned, beginning with Canelo in the valley between the Huachuca and the Patagonia Mountains. The first house was built in the 1870s by an American named Whitehill. It was a two-room adobe fortress with a single door and two loopholes in the wall for defense. Whitehill was killed not long after erecting this dwelling, and the structure itself, severely damaged by fire, was abandoned before the end of the decade.[14] In 1882 two Irish immigrant brothers, Pat and Tony O'Donnell, acquired the

Canelo, built in the 1870s and enlarged in the 80s.

property. In the 1890s they restored the existing part of the house and added two rooms and a shake roof to it.[15] Thus expanded, the Canelo ranch house stood for some forty years before a new owner, Tucson architect Frederick O. Knipe, enlarged it still farther, adding two flanking wings and a second story. The building now serves as headquarters for a bird sanctuary and ecological experiment station established on the property.[16]

Babocomari

The original ranch house at Babocomari, some fifteen miles north of Canelo, is the second of the little adobes. The great ranch, in a lovely setting along Babocomari Creek, was granted to Ignacio Elias and his sister Eulalia in 1832.[17] Boundary Commissioner John R. Bartlett in 1852 described it as "one of the largest establishments in Sonora" with "not less than 40,000 head of cattle roaming the length of the valley."[18] The California Volunteers occupied the site in 1866 and established a post named Camp Wallen at the headquarters. One of the soldiers described the large adobe building with its massive walled courtyard and its corner watch towers. The troops left in 1869 and the Apaches drove the ranchers out of the country. Cattle ran wild and buildings were abandoned until American settlers arrived and laid claim to the property.[19]

The old Babocomari ranch house was built in 1887. Its three rooms measured about fourteen by fourteen feet and were warmed by corner fireplaces. Wooden flooring was laid throughout. A simple lean-to kitchen was added to the north end of the living room and the other two rooms served as bedrooms. *Vigas* were exposed and the unadorned building with its flat roof and thick walls presented an authentic example of the Spanish-Mexican adobe.[20]

Babocomari, built in 1887, from the southeast.

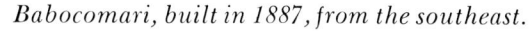

After passing through several hands, the ranch came into possession of Frank Cullen Brophy, its present owner. He added a fourth room, making an L, and expanded the kitchen to make a five-room house with bath for occupancy by one of the employees.[21]

Frank Brophy's new home, erected in 1941 close to the old house, harks back to the Spanish-Mexican frontier building tradition, though without any of the primitive quality which characterized it a century ago. Built upon a hillside overlooking some of Santa Cruz County's finest grazing lands, the house is constructed of the best materials. The adobe blocks used in the exterior walls were made near the house site, while the tile for window sills, porch floors and parapets came from Nogales. Cement was made with sand taken from Babocomari Creek, and the surrounding hills yielded the pale-pink rock used in construction. The house is built on two levels, following the slope of the land, and uses a line of contiguous rooms in order to gain the greatest exposure to the

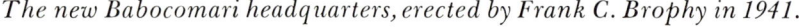

The new Babocomari headquarters, erected by Frank C. Brophy in 1941.

natural beauty of the countryside. The living room and bedrooms open to the southwest on a walled patio, forming a gently angled line. Windows and doors receive shade from a *portal* running the length of the façade.[22] The entire house has a simplicity of exterior profile which strongly recalls the native building idiom of southern Arizona, an impression furthered by the use of flat roofs and parapets and, within, of exposed *vigas* in the ceilings. At Babocomari, however, traditions are interpreted with an elegant hand, while modern technology has created a building of durability and structural excellence.

Bellota

Last of the little adobes is Bellota, northeast of Tucson near the old settlement of Redington. It was built in 1890 by Henry and Lem Redfield of New York who established the first permanent village in country where Indian attacks had made life impossible for many years. Soon Redfield cattle dotted the countryside and a farming and cattle-raising community developed. The Redfield brothers were content at first with a strip house consisting of two adjacent rooms, but a third room was added in line with the others and still later a fourth was built to form an ell on the north end — the development following an established Spanish-Mexican pattern. A shingled pitched roof now covers the original flat one.[23]

The late date of the Bellota Ranch house (1890) indicates that the occurrence of contiguous-room and L-shaped adobe houses was not limited to early times. Although refined structures were being built in both Spanish and American traditions by this time, the simpler forms continued to rise when economic or site conditions created a need.

97

Bellota, built in 1890 as a two-room adobe dwelling, now contains four rooms.

The headquarters of the Bellota ranch, constructed in 1933.

As was the case at Babocomari, an elegant modern structure replaced the old one. The new Bellota was built in 1933 for Swede Parker of Boston. Designed by Richard Morse and William Y. Peters, Tucson architects, it expresses the romanticized historicism of the twentieth-century Santa Fe school which came to predominate as the regional architecture of the Southwest, largely because of the efforts of the artist's colony at Taos. The Taos artists and their camp followers did much to popularize all aspects of the three cultures — Indian, Spanish and Anglo-American — of the Southwest. Thanks to them the new architectural taste looked to the Governor's Palace at Santa Fe and the multi-storied pueblo buildings for models rather than to products of the rough frontier common elsewhere on the northern fringes of the Spanish borderlands.[24] Since the building materials were the same in both traditions and since both employed such features as flat roofs, exposed beams, and flush fronts, the introduction of the Santa Fe mode did not constitute such a revolution as the importation of Victorian styles half a century earlier.

The builders of Bellota immersed themselves in the colonial style and the house shows a preponderant influence of the Santa Fe Governor's Palace. Wood for the *vigas* was brought from Oregon but other building materials were found at the site. The actual construction was carried on under the direction of a Mexican contractor skilled in working with adobe who moved to the ranch in order to give more minute attention to his task. In its completed state, the Bellota ranch house presents an outstanding example of fine craftsmanship enlightened by the study of architectural history.[25]

Sunset Hill

Another example of the invasion of New Mexican influence is Sunset Hill (Casa Rosada), sometimes known as New Rail X, which stands today on Sonoita Creek near the old Rail X headquarters. Designed in 1939 by Edmund Jacques of Illinois, the flat roof, parapet and massive walls recall the architecture of colonial Santa Fe.[26] The lower portions of the house are of rock, quarried at the site and fitted together by Mexican artisans so exactly that no mortar was necessary in construction. The second story, by contrast, is of reinforced concrete. The interior was finished by Bruce Cooper, a Santa Fe artist. With David Jeffcott, owner of Sunset Hill, Cooper spent months in Mexico making a special study of Spanish colonial architecture. Upon their return, Cooper designed all the interior tile work, while Terado, a Mexican craftsman from Alamos, Sonora, fashioned the iron work inside and out.[27]

Sunset Hill, an example of New Mexican architectural influence in Southern Arizona.

With the revival of native southwestern influences on southern Arizona ranch architecture, the cycle of taste had come full circle. Originally regional styles had evolved in response to primitive frontier conditions, preserving only as much of the European traditions of design and structure as could be accommodated in an isolated area where construction depended entirely upon locally available materials. With the ascendancy of the Anglo-American and the coming of the railroad, new styles appeared, and it became possible for builders first to adapt, then finally to drive out, the old. The resurrection a half century later of a distinctively regional architecture gave evidence of some romanticism, but it also marked awareness among a new generation of Southwesterners of the region's multicultural history and traditions. It was as fine a tribute to the past as the twentieth century could pay.

Credits and References

On the Sierra Bonita around the turn of the century. Colonel Hooker stands with his back to the camera.

THIS BOOK could not have been written without the assistance and cooperation of many individuals and many organizations.

Deepest gratitude is due to Gordon Heck, Professor of Architecture at the University of Arizona, under whom the study was begun and whose guidance has been invaluable. The plans and drawings were made by him.

John Bret Harte's taste and skill as an editor gave the book its shape and helped to establish its tone.

Richard S. Caldwell, New Orleans architect, and Hugh Morrison of Dartmouth College (author of *Early American Architecture*) gave generous help.

Special thanks go to Cecil L. Chase of the Bancroft Library, Berkeley, California; Robert B. Gates, Santa Barbara Historical Society; R. C. Johnson, The Newberry Library, Chicago; Louise Lutz, The Art Institute of Chicago; Harold L. Myers, Pennsylvania Historical and Museum Commission, Harrisburg, Pennsylvania; James Yeingst, Elizabethtown College, Elizabethtown, Pennsylvania.

The Arizona Historical Society and its personnel have provided indispensable assistance. The library staff helped continuously in research. Sidney B. Brinckerhoff, Director, and the Publications Committee arranged for the contemporary photographs of the houses and commissioned Louis Bencze to make them. The editorial staff — C. L. Sonnichsen, A. Tracy Row and Sybil Ellinwood — worked tirelessly with text and references. Mr. Row designed the book.

Finally, a special debt must be acknowledged to the present owners of the ranch houses, the descendants of the original builders, and those who have been associated with the ranch properties through the years. I am grateful to each one for giving generously of his time in repeated interviews and letters and for opening the houses to me. For their sakes it should be added that with the exception of the three guest ranches— Tanque Verde, Circle Z (old Sanford) and La Osa—the houses are private, year-round residences and not open to visitors.

I want to give special recognition to the Walter Kolbe family who maintained the 23,000-acre Rail X as a working cattle ranch and guest resort for nearly twenty years. The Kolbes lived in the sprawling Rail X (c. 1880) adobe and housed their guests in the luxurious Sunset Hill mansion, high above the spread. Their children, including Arizona Congressman Jim Kolbe (R., District 5), resided in the old house and participated in all the ranching and guest operations.

JANET A. STEWART

Photographs from the archives of the Arizona Historical Society appear on pages vi, 14, 22, 46 and 64; from the Forbes Collection on 16; from the Henry and Albert Buehman Memorial Collection on 32, 42, 85 and 102.

The photograph on page 74 is from the Kinder family collection; on page 88 from the La Osa Ranch collection.

The floor plans and sketches on pages 7, 21, 27, 35, 53, 60, 68 and 81 are by Gordon Heck.

The map on page 10 is by Donald Bufkin.

Photographs by Louis Bencze, taken in 1973, appear throughout the book.

NOTES

Birth of A Style

[1] Ralph Adams Cram, introduction to Winsor Soulé, *Spanish Farm Houses and Minor Public Buildings* (New York: Architectural Publishing Company, 1923), pp. 2, 3; David Talbot Rice, *Islamic Art* (New York: Frederick A. Praeger, 1965), pp. 19–24.

[2] Serge Chermayeff, *Community Privacy* (Garden City: Doubleday, 1963), p. 181; Rexford Newcomb, *Spanish Colonial Architecture in the United States* (New York: J. J. Augustin, 1937), pp. 36–37.

[3] Randolph W. Sexton, *Spanish Influence on American Architecture* (New York: Brentano's, 1927), pp. 31–33; George Kubler, *Mexican Architecture of the Sixteenth Century* (New Haven: Yale University Press, 1948), Vol. 1, p. 171.

[4] Alan Gowans, *Images of American Living* (Philadelphia: Lippincott, 1964), p. 4; Amos Rapoport, *House Form and Culture* (Englewood Cliffs: Prentice-Hall, 1969), pp. 2, 5.

[5] Sherban Cantacuzino, *European Domestic Architecture* (London: Studio Vista, 1969), pp. 22–25; Kubler, *Mexican Architecture*, p. 188.

[6] Sylvanus Baxter, *Spanish Colonial Architecture in America* (Boston: J. B. Miller, 1902), Vol. 2, p. 130; Trent Elwood Sanford, *The Story of Architecture in Mexico* (New York: W. W. Norton, 1947), pp. 262–263.

[7] Trent Elwood Sanford, *The Architecture of the Southwest* (New York: W. W. Norton, 1950), p. 126. Baxter, *Spanish Colonial Architecture*, Vol. 1, pp. 36, 136.

[8] Building Research Advisory Board, *Housing and Building in Hot and Dry-Hot Climates* (Washington: National Academy of Sciences, 1935), pp. 34, 111.

[9] Victor Olgyay, *Design with Climate* (Princeton University Press, 1963), p. 8; David C. Mackie, ed., *Historic Architecture of Tucson* (City of Tucson, 1971), pp. 191–193, 196.

[10] Hilario Gallego, Memoirs, Ms., dictated to Edith Kitt, April 22, 1926, in the Arizona Historical Society, Tucson, Arizona.

[11] Kubler, *Mexican Architecture*, pp. 201–202.

[12] Cornelius C. Smith, "Some Unpublished History of the Southwest: An Old Diary Found in Mexico," *Arizona Historical Review*, Vol. 6 (January, 1935), pp. 60–61.

[13] James M. Fitch, *Architecture and the Aesthetics of Plenty* (New York: Columbia University Press, 1961), p. 4.

[14] Mackie, ed., *Historic Architecture,* pp. 4, 9.

[15] Wallace W. Elliott, ed., *History of Arizona Territory* (San Francisco: W. W. Elliott, Publisher, 1884), p. 265.

[16] Herbert Eugene Bolton, *The Rim of Christendom* (New York: Macmillan, 1936), p. 589.

[17] Bert Haskett, "Early History of the Cattle Industry in Arizona," *Arizona Historical Review,* Vol. 6 (October, 1935), pp. 3–5; Ray H. Mattison, "Early Spanish and Mexican Settlements in Arizona," *New Mexico Historical Review,* Vol. 21 (October, 1946), pp. 285–287. Spanish ruling under the Law of the West (Sinaloa, Sonora and southern Arizona) decreed a land grant of four *sitios* (one square league) to each grantee for cattle ranching purposes. The grantee was required to prove that he was using the land solely for cattle raising by the immediate stocking of his property. The boundaries were identified only by stone markers, and this led to later problems over water rights, wandering of cattle and land disputes. Mexican settlement in the nineteenth century frequently meant reoccupation of the seventeenth-century locations and earlier Indian settlements. Between 1820 and 1830 the country was stocked with thousands of head of cattle, but Apache depredations of 1830–1843 forced the settlers to abandon their haciendas and flee to walled cities for safety. By 1880 most of the Mexican ranch sites had been reestablished by Americans and cattle raising had become a viable industry. For Private Land Claim settlements of southern Arizona's ranchers, see *Report of the Governor of Arizona to the Secretary of the Interior, 1893* (Washington: Government Printing Office, 1893), pp. 340–341.

[18] Haskett, "Early History of the Cattle Industry," p. 19; *Report of the Governor of Arizona to the Secretary of the Interior, 1896* (Washington: Government Printing Office, 1896), p. 21.

[19] Cornelius C. Smith, "Tucson: The Old Pueblo," *Arizona Historical Review,* Vol. 3 (April, 1930), p. 13.

[20] Ray Brandes, *Frontier Military Posts of Arizona* (Globe: Dale Stuart King, 1960), pp. 8–10.

[21] *Arizona Miner* (Prescott), December 7, 1877; J. J. Wagoner, *History of the Cattle Industry in Southern Arizona, 1540–1940* (Tucson: University of Arizona Press, 1952), p. 36.

[22] Clarence W. Gordon, "Report on Cattle, Sheep, and Swine, Supplementary to Livestock on Farms in 1880," *Tenth Census of the United States, 1880* (Washington: Government Printing Office, 1883), p. 93.

[23] Haskett, "Early History of the Cattle Industry," pp. 16, 23; Joseph Amasa Munk, *Arizona Sketches* (New York: Grafton Press, 1905), p. 74.

[24] Isabel Fathauer, interview with Janet A. Stewart, Tucson, April 14, 1968; Gordon, "Report on Cattle," pp. 96–97.

[25] Walter P. Webb, *The Great Plains* (Boston: Ginn and Company, 1931), pp. 228, 243, 274; Robert Humphrey Forbes, *The Penningtons* (Lancaster: The New Era Printing Company, 1919), p. 6.

[26] Rupert Norval Richardson, *The Greater Southwest* (Glendale: Arthur H. Clark, 1935), pp. 338–340.

[27] Gordon, "Report on Cattle," p. 95; *The Arizona Daily Star* (Tucson), October 15, 1936.

[28] *Report of the Secretary of the Interior,* Vol. 3 (Washington: Government Printing Office, 1893), p. 21; Webb, *The Great Plains,* pp. 306–308.

[29] *Tombstone Prospector,* December 17, 1887.

[30] *Ibid.,* April 15, 1887; J. J. Wagoner, "Overstocking of the Ranges in Southern Arizona during the 1870s and 1880s," *Arizoniana,* Vol. 2 (Spring, 1961), p. 145.

[31] *Report of the Governor of Arizona to the Secretary of the Interior, 1896* (Washington: Government Printing Office, 1896), p. 23.

[32] *Ibid.,* pp. 22, 23; Haskett, "Early History of the Cattle Industry," p. 39.

[33] *Report of the Governor of Arizona to the Secretary of the Interior, 1889* (Washington: Government Printing Office, 1889), p. 13. Wagoner, *History of the Cattle Industry,* pp. 53, 55.

Frontier Fortresses

[1] Bert Haskett, "Early History of the Cattle Industry in Arizona," *Arizona Historical Review,* Vol. 6 (October, 1935), p. 18; Ray H. Mattison, "Early Spanish and Mexican Settlements in Arizona," *New Mexico Historical Review,* Vol. 21 (October, 1946), p. 296. Pete Kitchen ranched on Canoa lands north of Tubac (the Canoa grant dated from 1821) from 1855 until he was driven out by Apaches in 1861. He was a merchant in Sonora until the end of the Civil War.

[2] Frank C. Lockwood, "Pete Kitchen: Arizona Pioneer Rifleman and Ranchman," *Arizona Historical Review,* Vol. 1 (April, 1928), p. 76.

[3] *Ibid.,* p. 81; Frank C. Lockwood, "One Thousand Acres on Potrero Creek," *The Arizona Daily Star,* November 3, 1940.

[4] Unidentified Mss. and undated newspaper articles, Pete Kitchen Clipbook, Arizona Historical Society, Tucson, Arizona.

[5] Lockwood, "Pete Kitchen," p. 79.

[6] Gilbert Proctor, interview with Janet A. Stewart, Pete Kitchen Ranch, November 11, 1968.

[7] *Ibid.*, March 3, 1969; Lockwood, "Pete Kitchen," p. 80.

[8] Gilbert Proctor, interview, March 3, 1969.

[9] *Ibid.*, November 11, 1968.

[10] Elmer E. Davis, "Where the Ancient and Modern Meet — Tanque Verde Ranch," *Progressive Arizona and the Great Southwest,* Vol. 7 (September, 1928), pp. 22–23; "Rancho Tanque Verde," *The Arizona Daily Star,* February 20, 1957; "Emilio Carrillo," Hayden file, Arizona Historical Society.

[11] James P. Converse, interview with JAS, Tanque Verde Ranch, July 22, 1968.

[12] *Ibid.*, August 21, 1968.

[13] Reuben Underhill, *Cowhides to Golden Fleece* (Stanford University Press, 1939), p. 14; James Converse, interview, August 21, 1968.

[14] *Arizona Daily Star,* February 15, 1908, February 24, 1957; *Tucson Daily Citizen,* February 14, 1908; Davis, "Tanque Verde Ranch," p. 23.

[15] *The Arizona Daily Star,* February 22, 1935, June 28, 1957; James Converse, interview, August 21, 1968.

Regional Style Matures

[1] Henry Hooker left his native New Hampshire at twenty-five for California, where he started a mercantile business. The combined store and residence burned in 1866 and he left shortly thereafter for Arizona. *Los Angeles Evening News,* December 5, 1907; Roscoe G. Willson, *Pioneer Cattlemen of Arizona* (Phoenix: Valley National Bank, 1951), Vol. 1, p. 25.

[2] Jessie P. Hooker, letter to Janet A. Stewart, January 30, 1971; Joseph Amasa Munk, *Arizona Sketches* (New York: The Grafton Press, 1905), p. 101.

[3] Rupert Norval Richardson, *The Greater Southwest* (Glendale: Arthur H. Clark Company, 1935), pp. 331, 340–341; Gertrude Hill, "Henry Clay Hooker: King of the Sierra Bonita," *Arizoniana,* Vol. 2 (Winter, 1961), p. 13. Henry Hooker gave some of his inferior cattle to the Indians to satisfy their needs. The house itself was never attacked, but within a twenty-year period forty men were killed and many cattle were stolen. James H. McClintock, *Arizona* (Chicago: S. J. Clark, 1916), Vol. 2, p. 447.

[4] Hooker may well have been familiar with the New England "hollow square" village of the eighteenth century. See John W. Reps, *The Making of Urban*

America (Princeton University Press, 1965), p. 32. During his years of dealing with the military he observed the advantage of the fortified quad (Jessie P. Hooker, interview with JAS, Tucson, January 28, 1971). Both building patterns were compatible with the Spanish-Mexican patio plan used at Sierra Bonita.

[5]*Arizona Daily Citizen,* June 6, 1874: "There are fifty horses, four corrals, three of adobe and one plank; the largest will hold three thousand head of cattle."

[6]Wallace W. Elliott, ed., *History of Arizona Territory* (San Francisco: W. W. Elliott, Publisher, 1884), p. 235.

[7]Jessie P. Hooker, interview. The majority of the fireplaces have been sealed and their exact location can be determined only by breaking into the walls.

[8]Jessie P. Hooker, letter to JAS, February 3, 1969.

[9]*Arizona Daily Citizen,* June 5, 1875.

[10]Charles Whelan, interview with JAS, Sierra Bonita Ranch, March 8, 1969. Adobes of the original corrals were made from clay at the site of an Indian burial ground located near the ranch house.

[11]Jessie P. Hooker, "Four Generations of Hookers," *Arizona Cattlelog,* Vol. 5 (December, 1949), p. 34.

[12]*Arizona Daily Citizen,* March 21, 1879.

[13]Elliott, *History of Arizona,* pp. 185, 298.

[14]Richardson, *Greater Southwest,* pp. 331, 340–341; *Arizona Citizen,* December 19, 1874.

[15]Hill, "Henry Clay Hooker," p. 14.

[16]Earle R. Forrest, "The Fabulous Sierra Bonita," *The Journal of Arizona History,* Vol. 6 (Autumn, 1965), p. 132.

[17]Forrestine Cooper Hooker, Hooker's novelist daughter-in-law, lived at the Sierra Bonita ranch house from the time of her marriage in 1886. In *The Long, Dim Trail* (New York: Knopf, 1921), pp. 124–126, she described a dwelling matching the Hooker residence in every detail with "windmills that supplied the troughs and ponds with water," box stalls from which "sleek heads of handsome horses peered curiously," a courtyard eighty feet square with porches on the sides, the windmill in the center of the court and red Navajo rugs in a low-ceilinged living room lit by "long French windows." It may be that in her time mail-order casements were built into the walls facing the patio.

[18]Jessie P. Hooker, interview.

The Triumph of Expansion

[1] Pima, Santa Cruz and Cochise Counties. The spread covered more than one thousand square miles.

[2] The oldest part of the structure, the Mexican adobe, is remarkably well built. The corners are nearly square and the room sizes are almost identical. The builder must have been a qualified craftsman. Additions are not nearly so well constructed.

[3] Harry L. Heffner, letter, February 5, 1954, to Mary Boice Souders, in Empire Ranch Papers, 1874–1944, Special Collections, University of Arizona. Heffner was employed at the ranch from 1893 to 1907, serving as foreman during much of that time.

[4] 1876 is the latest date for the adobe house, but the Mexican building may have been built before E. N. Fish's purchase of the ranch in 1870.

[5] *The Arizona Daily Star,* October 15, 1936.

[6] *An Englishman's Arizona: The Ranching Letters of Herbert Hislop, 1876–1878* (Tucson: Overland Press, 1965), pp. x, xiii. During his stay in America, Herbert Hislop wrote a series of letters to his sister, Amy Tate, in London.

[7] Reminiscences of Edward L. Vail, Ms., Arizona Historical Society, Tucson, Arizona.

[8] *Ibid.; An Englishman's Arizona,* p. 70.

[9] *An Englishman's Arizona,* p. ix.

[10] *Ibid.,* p. xvii.

[11] *Arizona Citizen,* August 26, 1876.

[12] Herbert Hislop, letter to Nathan Vail, July 18, 1876, Vail Collection, Arizona Historical Society.

[13] Heffner, letter to Mary Boice Souders; Harry Heffner, interview with Charles Pickerell, Tucson, June 4, 1960, Special Collections, University of Arizona.

[14] *An Englishman's Arizona,* pp. xii, 29, 45.

[15] *Ibid.,* pp. 38, 39, 50.

[16] *Ibid.,* pp. 43, 45, 54.

[17] Reminiscences of Edward L. Vail.

[18] *An Englishman's Arizona,* pp. xii, 61.

[19] *Arizona Daily Star,* November 23, 1944.

[20] *An Englishman's Arizona,* pp. xi, xii, 56.

[21]*Ibid.*, p. xii; J. J. Wagoner, *History of the Cattle Industry in Southern Arizona, 1540–1940* (Tucson: University of Arizona Press, 1952), p. 41.

[22]*The Arizona Daily Star,* October 15, 1936; Patrick Hamilton, *The Resources of Arizona* (Tucson; Piñon Press, 1966), p. 46. The Empire District, about twenty miles below Tucson, had as its largest and richest vein the Total Wreck that was "more than fifty miles wide and assayed from $10 to $500 per ton of both gold and silver."

[23] Heffner, interview with Charles Pickerell.

[24] Heffner, letter to Mary Boice Souders.

[25] Robin Grey, interview with Janet A. Stewart, Empire Ranch, February 25, 1968. A rise occurs between the bedroom and family room to fit the terrain.

[26] Heffner, letter to Mary Boice Souders.

[27] Wagoner, *History of the Cattle Industry,* p. 46.

New Styles

[1] Jeanette Roll Riggs, *Our Eldorado* (privately printed, 1957), pp. 31, 33.

[2] A. T. Steele, "The Lady Boss of Faraway Ranch," *The Saturday Evening Post,* Vol. 241 (March 15, 1958), p. 132.

[3] Lillian Erickson Riggs, interview with Janet A. Stewart, Faraway Ranch, September 14, 1968.

[4] Lillian Erickson Riggs, letter to JAS, June 30, 1968.

[5] Riggs, interview, September 14, 1968; Riggs, letter to JAS, July 31, 1968. Neil Erickson utilized three carpentry and building manuals in constructing Faraway, but the titles and authors are no longer known. He practiced his carpentry at Bisbee, Willcox and Fort Huachuca, using fine tools ordered from specialty houses.

[6] Riggs, interview, July 11, 1968; For the "growing house," see Hugh Morrison, *Early American Architecture* (New York: Oxford University Press, 1952), p. 52; Neil Erickson's North European ancestry influenced his verticality in building and his use of wood wherever possible. But also, the higher altitude and resulting cooler climate would have determined a house form different from that of the desert floor. Just before Faraway was built, twenty-two inches of rain fell at nearby Fort Grant as against ten inches on the desert. The greater rainfall called for a pitched or hipped roof rather than the Spanish-Mexican flat roof. James H. McClintock, *Arizona* (Chicago: S. J. Clarke, 1916), Vol. 3, p. 6; Allen Erwin, *The Southwest of John H. Slaughter* (Glendale: Arthur H. Clark, 1965), pp. 59–62, 75–87.

[7]Ray H. Mattison, "Early Spanish and Mexican Settlements in Arizona," *New Mexico Historical Review,* Vol. 31 (October, 1946), p. 304.

[8]Rex C. Gerald, *Spanish Presidios of the Late Eighteenth Century* (Santa Fe: Museum of New Mexico, 1968), pp. 14, 21, drawing p. 29. In 1775 troops were moved to the San Bernardino Valley and a presidio was constructed according to the *Reglamento.* See Hugh Morrison, *Early American Architecture* (New York: Oxford University Press, 1952), p. 241. The presidio was built of adobe masonry with two bastions, inner quarters for the men and a chapel. *The Arizona Daily Star,* Feb. 19, 1938.

[9]Julius Froebel, *Seven Years Travel in Central America, Northern Mexico, and the Far West of the United States* (London: R. C. Bentley, 1859), pp. 486–488.

[10]John Russell Bartlett, *Personal Narrative of Explorations and Incidents* (New York: Appleton, 1854), Vol. 1, p. 255.

[11]H. M. T. Powell, *The Santa Fe Trail to California, 1849–1852* (San Francisco: Book Club of California, 1931), pp. 126–127.

[12]Bert Haskett, "Early History of the Cattle Industry in Arizona," *Arizona Historical Review,* Vol. 6 (October, 1935), p. 30.

[13]McClintock, *Arizona,* Vol. 3, p. 6; Memoirs of Cora Viola Slaughter, Ms., Arizona Historical Society, Tucson; *Bisbee Daily Review,* April 22, 1934.

[14]Erwin, *John H. Slaughter,* pp. 154–158; Allen Erwin, letter to JAS, March 24, 1973.

[15]Allen Erwin, letters to JAS, April 14 and June 5, 1973.

[16]Adeline Green Parks, letter to JAS, January 31, 1969.

[17]*Ibid.,* February 1, 1969.

[18]Ben Williams, interview with JAS, Douglas, January 30, 1968.

[19]Ben Williams, letter to JAS, July 23, 1968.

[20]Erwin, *John H. Slaughter,* pp. 293–294.

[21]Drury Blakeley Alexander, *Texas Homes of the Nineteenth Century* (The University of Texas Press, 1966), pp. 12–13, 16. German pioneers brought the dog-run house type with them from the Carolinas to their new settlements in south Texas. This example reinforced the Slaughter's previous experience with the house type when they built their family home in Friotown, near San Antonio, ca. 1870. John Slaughter adapted the style to Arizona's frontier conditions in building the schoolhouse at San Bernardino.

[22]A. G. Parks, letter, February 1, 1969.

[23] Bernice Cosulich, "Romance and Drama in Life of Tombstone Sheriff's Widow," *Arizona Daily Star,* February 19, 1938.

[24] A. G. Parks, letter, January 31, 1969.

Eastern Invasion

[1] On March 25, 1884, Colin Cameron wrote to prospective investor Alexander Fulford of Bel Air, Maryland: "We have a tract of country thirty or thirty-five miles wide by fifty long — it is a principality. We started with a capital of $150,000 but will on my return east increase it to $250,000 — 300 shares, $500 each. It cost us less than 30 cents per acre and in ten years will be in demand at $10.00." Cameron had investigated seven states before deciding on the spread "selected by United States Army Officers as the finest in all this country in years gone by." San Rafael Cattle Company Papers, Special Collections, University of Arizona (cited hereafter as SRCC Papers).

[2] Brewster Cameron letters, September 4 and November 24, 1886, to Alexander Fulford, in SRCC Papers.

[3] Richard Caldwell, letter to Janet A. Stewart, October 21, 1968. Hugh Morrison, *Early American Architecture* (New York: Oxford University Press, 1952), pp. 259, 263–4; Building Research Advisory Board, *Housing and Building in Hot and Dry-Hot Climates* (Washington, D. C.: National Academy of Sciences, 1935), pp. 76–77.

[4] Erwin Stanley Bradley, *Simon Cameron, Lincoln's Secretary of War* (Philadelphia: University of Pennsylvania Press, 1966), pp. 412–413, 417; Gail M. Gibson, letter to JAS, September 10, 1969; Harold L. Myers, letter to JAS, May 29, 1973; James Yeingst, letters to JAS, August 4 and August 23, 1973. There is excellent coverage of Simon Cameron and his son, James Donald Cameron, in *The Encyclopedia Americana* (New York: Americana Corporation, 1960), Vol. 5, pp. 263–264.

[5] Brewster Cameron, letter, September 15, 1884, to Alexander Fulford, SRCC Papers; Brewster Cameron, letter to Senator Cameron, September 11, 1884, SRCC Papers; "S.A.H.," letter, n.d., to unknown, with drawing, SRCC Papers; Alice Cameron Edgerton Ms., 1973, pp. 4, 32, 41, 45, 46 (hereafter cited as Edgerton Ms.).

[6] Alice Cameron Edgerton, letter to JAS, September 21, 1973; Hugh Morrison, *American Architecture,* p. 518, explains that in Pennsylvania country houses such a wing did not obstruct the view from the central hallway, but left a vista through the back door to the gardens.

[7] Brewster Cameron, letter to Senator J. Donald Cameron, September 11, 1888, SRCC Papers; Mary Ann Kinder, interview with JAS, Tucson, September 9, 1969; Edgerton Ms., pp. 4, 32, 40, 46.

[8] The Settlers Protective Association, letter, April 1, 1899, to Colin Cameron; Edgerton, Ms., p. 4; *Arizona Republican* (Phoenix), January 7, 1900.

[9] *Arizona Republican,* November 10, 1900; Edgerton Ms., p. 4.

[10] Susan B. Judice, letter to JAS, September 18, 1968; Jenephier Nevers, letter to JAS, October 18, 1968.

[11] Robert B. Gates, letter to JAS, March 7, 1972; Reuben L. Underhill, *From Cowhides to Golden Fleece* (Stanford University Press, 1939), pp. 18, 53.

[12] Thomas Tileston Waterman, *The Early Architecture of North Carolina* (Chapel Hill: University of North Carolina Press, 1947), p. 47; Fred Kniffen, "Folk Housing: Key to Diffusion," *Annals of the Association of American Geographers,* Vol. 50 (December, 1965), p. 571.

[13] Alan Gowans, *Images of American Living* (Philadelphia: J. B. Lippincott Company, 1964), p. 340; Douglas D. Martin, *The Lamp in the Desert* (Tucson: University of Arizona Press, 1960), p. 34.

[14] John Leece, "Determinants Study, Phase 1, The San Rafael Ranch," Ms. prepared for the College of Architecture, University of Arizona, October, 1966, pp. 1–3. Florence Greene Sharp, interview with JAS, San Rafael Ranch, January 4, 1969; Jane Greene Sharp, interview with JAS, San Rafael Ranch, January 4, 1969.

[15] Edgerton Ms., pp. 5–7, 9; Alice Cameron Edgerton, letters to JAS, March 28, April 28, August 1, 1973. Mary Cameron Wakefield, interviews with JAS, Tucson, November 16, 1969, and January 10, 1970.

[16] Edgerton Ms., pp. 4, 7, 8, 20; Mary Ann Kinder, interview.

[17] Roscoe Willson, *Pioneer and Well Known Cattlemen of Arizona* (Phoenix: Valley National Bank, 1956), Vol. 2, p. 28. In 1825 Don Ramón Romero, a resident of the presidio at Santa Cruz, received the title to four *sitios* of land called San Rafael de la Zanja situated between the Huachuca and Patagonia Mountains. Much of the grant was within the presidio's jurisdiction and later included the mining camps of Harshaw and Washington in the Patagonia Mountain Range. See James H. McClintock, *Arizona* (Chicago: S. J. Clark Publishing Company, 1916) Vol. 3, p. 529; Jane Abigail Wayland, "Experiment on the Santa Cruz: Colin Cameron's San Rafael Cattle Company, 1882–1893," unpublished Master's thesis, University of Arizona, 1964.

[18] Edgerton Ms., pp. 13, 19, 38; Florence Greene Sharp, Jane Greene Sharp, interviews with JAS, San Rafael Ranch, January 4, 1969.

Big Adobes, Little Adobes and Modern Adaptations

[1] Lee Zinsmeister, "The Old Sanford Ranch," *Westward Ho,* Vol. 1 (November-December, 1929), pp. 16, 41–45; Don Alonzo Sanford wrote in his Book of Records, now in the collection of Louise McKee Summers, in July, 1874, that "the ranch was already stocked with cattle" and that the brothers "had bargained with men at E. N. Fish's to make adobes." Perhaps E. N. Fish was then building the large adobe at the Empire Ranch.

[2] Sanford, Book of Records; Bertha Sanford Miller, "Reminiscences," Ms., Arizona Historical Society. Denton was joined by his brother Don Alonzo and other members of the family who homesteaded along Sonoita Creek until they controlled the water supply of a ten-mile strip of the fertile lands.

[3] Louise Summers, interview with Janet A. Stewart, Tucson, October 2, 1973; Frank Fendig, interviews with JAS, Circle Z Guest Ranch, March 4, July 31, 1973.

[4] Louise Summers, interview. There were two small adobes below the ranch house. One was for grain storage and the other was used as quarters for workers who built the Santa Fe Railroad during the summer of 1882 (David Myrick, letter to JAS, August 6, 1973). The buildings were fronted by an adobe wall three feet high, and an adobe corral extended far to the rear of the buildings. Across the creek, to the southeast, was the Milk Ranch with a two-room adobe for work rooms and storage, all the buildings forming a large-scale ranch complex.

[5] *Arizona Daily Star,* May 4, 1883; Bernard L. Fontana, "Johnny Ward's Ranch," *Kiva,* Vol. 28 (October-December, 1962), pp. 11–16. Sonoita was an early *visita* of Father Kino, see Herbert Eugene Bolton, *The Rim of Christendom* (New York: Macmillan Company, 1936), p. 594. In the nineteenth century the Herreras family was driven from the land by the Apache raids of 1833 and 1836.

[6] Zinsmeister, "Old Sanford Ranch," p. 45.

[7] Helene May, interview with JAS, Crittenden, October 1, 1970. The living room, dining room and kitchen were on the west side, and two bedrooms and the ranch office extended along the east side. This room arrangement indicates that the hallway was during some periods used as living space.

[8] Edward M. Jeffcott, interview with JAS, Nogales, Arizona, September 23, 1970. Brewster Cameron wrote to Alexander Fulford on September 15, 1884 (see chapter on San Rafael), that he and Colin had bought their ranch from R. R. Richardson for $5,000 in "stock in San Rafael Cattle Company and the balance in cash. He has since bought another ranch [Rail X] and the Fort Crittenden reservation just north of us" (San Rafael Cattle Company Papers, Special Collections, University of Arizona).

[9] Hulda Ashburn Laney, interviews with JAS, Nogales, Sonora, October 2, 5, 1970. A break in the foundation of the original front (west) façade indicates presence of the doorway. Orientation of the house was reversed during the 1915 alterations when the carcass was stuccoed and the eastern wings were added. The house, originally flat-roofed, may have been built when Thomas Hughes started the ranch in 1869. Conjecturally, Rollin Rice Richardson, an Easterner from Pennsylvania, added the pitched roof and the bay window after he bought the ranch from Hughes in 1883 and named the property the Pennsylvania Ranch. In 1901 the property was sold to Vail, Gates and Ashburn (Roscoe G. Willson, *Pioneer Cattlemen of Arizona,* Phoenix: Valley National Bank, 1951, Vol. 1, p. 24); *Report of the Governor of Arizona to the Secretary of the Interior, 1896* (Washington: Government Printing Office, 1896), p. 21.

[10] The original Mexican land grant of Arivaca was awarded to Tomás and Fernando Ortíz who built "a ranch house and outbuildings, all substantially built" (Survey Book 921, 922, December 9, 1886, in possession of William J. Mitchell, La Osa Ranch; interview with JAS, December 5, 1970). The Ortíz family apparently built the two-room adobe at La Osa (Antonio L. Aros, interview with JAS, Tucson, October 10, 1970).

[11] Ebenezer Buckingham, *Solomon Sturges and His Descendants* (New York: Grafton Press, 1907), pp. 58–60, 72; William Spencer Sturges' father, Shelton Sturges, a Chicago banker and merchandiser, was in the process of acquiring the Ortíz Ranch, which he had already stocked, at the time of his death in 1888. William Sturges took over La Osa, married Leonor de Savin in 1892, sold the spread to Lyman Wakefield and Edward L. Vail (of the Empire holdings) nine years later, and settled in Arivaca. The *Arizona Daily Star,* August 28, 1889, described the ranch as "one of the most beautiful tracts in Arizona with several acres under fine cultivation" and "a fine residence, handsomely furnished, and the full quota of outbuildings. . . . It is a paradise, and the hospitality of Mr. Sturges is synonomous with the name and reputation of La Osa."

[12] R. M. Pacheco, interviews with JAS, Tucson, September 25, October 10, 26, 1970. Pacheco enlarged the main house in 1929 when he was commissioned to remodel the buildings for use as a guest ranch. He built the large main patio and its eastern border of rooms. At this time Pacheco located *vigas* which were previously covered by a ceiling. He also added the parapet, thus disguising the slightly pitched roof.

[13] Nellie Jenkins, interview with JAS, Tucson, November 28, 1970. Miss Jenkins and her brother Richard purchased the ranch in 1931 and added the smaller patio on the north side with its adjoining guest rooms. As the guest ranch expanded its operations, they added several detached cottages.

[14] John McCarty Ms. in the Arizona Historical Society, Tucson, Arizona.

[15] Kathleen O'Donnell, "Patrick O'Donnell Recalls Old Days on Arizona Ranch," *The Arizona Daily Star,* July 6, 1930.

[16] *The Arizona Daily Star,* September 20, 1973.

[17] L. A. Boedecker, letters to Edith Kitt, December 9, 21, 1930, Arizona Historical Society; Ray Mattison, "Early Spanish and Mexican Settlements in Arizona," *New Mexico Historical Review,* Vol. 21 (October, 1946), pp. 313–314.

[18] John Russell Bartlett, *Personal Narrative of Explorations and Incidents* (New York: Appleton, 1854), Vol. 1, p. 393; Herbert Eugene Bolton, *The Rim of Christendom* (New York: Macmillan, 1936), p. 594.

[19] Ray Brandes, *Frontier Military Posts of Arizona* (Globe: Dale Stuart King, 1960), p. 73; L. R. Bailey, ed., *The A. B. Gray Report* (Los Angeles: Westernlore Press, 1963), p. 77.

[20] Frank Cullen Brophy, letters to JAS, August 29, 1968, January 28, 1969; Fern B. Collie, letter to JAS, March 9, 1974; Richard G. Schaus, "Edward Bert Perrin," *Arizona Cattlelog,* Vol. 25 (August, 1968), back cover and p. 40. A man named Choate built the adobe house, thinking the land was open, and Dr. Edward B. Perrin and his brother Robert purchased the property one year later, in 1888.

[21] Frank C. Brophy, letter to JAS, February 11, 1971.

[22] *Ibid.,* April 25, 1974. The land slope allowed building bedrooms beneath the northside kitchen and sitting porch.

[23] Katherine Reeve, interview with JAS, Bellota, August 25, 1970; Josephine T. Reeve, letter to JAS, March 14, 1973.

[24] Hugh Morrison, *Early American Architecture* (New York: Oxford University Press, 1952), pp. 184–186.

[25] Richard A. Morse, interview with JAS, Tucson, October 4, 1970. The adobe bricks were originally exposed and were stuccoed twenty years later by the owners.

[26] The house was completed in 1945.

[27] Edward Jeffcott, letter to JAS, September 3, 1970, and interview, Nogales, Arizona, October 1, 1970. The large dining room, offices and a three-car garage are located on the lower floor.

BIBLIOGRAPHY

Alexander, Drury Blakeley, *Texas Homes of the Nineteenth Century*. Austin: The University of Texas Press, 1966.

Bancroft, Hubert Howe, *History of Arizona and New Mexico, 1530–1888, Works*, Vol. 17. San Francisco: The History Company, 1889.

Bailey, L. R., editor, *Survey of a Route on the 32nd Parallel for the Texas Western Railroad, 1854: The A. B. Gray Report, and including the Reminiscences of Peter R. Brady who accompanied the expedition*. Los Angeles: Westernlore Press, 1963.

Bartlett, John Russell, *Personal Narrative of Explorations and Incidents*, Vol. 1. New York: D. Appleton & Company, 1854.

Baxter, Sylvanus, *Spanish Colonial Architecture in America*, Vol. 2. Boston: J. B. Miller, 1902.

Bolton, Herbert Eugene, *The Rim of Christendom*. New York: The Macmillan Company, 1936.

Bradley, Erwin Stanley, *Simon Cameron, Lincoln's Secretary of War: A Political Biography*. Philadelphia: University of Pennsylvania Press, 1966.

Brandes, Ray, *Frontier Military Posts of Arizona*. Globe: Dale Stuart King, 1960.

Buckingham, Ebenezer, compiler, *Solomon Sturges and His Descendants: A Memoir and a Genealogy*. New York: The Grafton Press, 1907.

Building Research and Advisory Board, *Housing and Building in Hot and Dry-Hot Climates*. Washington, D. C.: National Academy of Sciences, 1935.

Cameron, Brewster, letters, September 11, 1884, to Senator Simon Cameron; September 15, 1884, September 4, November 24, 1886, to Alexander Fulford. San Rafael Cattle Company Papers, Special Collections, University of Arizona Library.

Cameron, Colin, letter, March 25, 1884, to Alexander Fulford. San Rafael Cattle Company Papers, Special Collections, University of Arizona Library.

Cantacuzino, Sherban, *European Domestic Architecture*. London: Studio Vista Limited, 1969.

Chermayeff, Serge, *Community Privacy*. Garden City: Doubleday and Company, 1963.

Cosulich, Bernice, "Romance and Drama in Life of Tombstone Sheriff's Widow," *The Arizona Daily Star* (Tucson), February 19, 1938.

Cram, Ralph Adams, introduction to Winsor Soulé, *Spanish Farm Houses and Minor Public Buildings.* New York: Architectural Publishing Company, 1924.

Elliott, Wallace W., editor, *History of Arizona Territory.* San Francisco: Wallace W. Elliott and Company, 1884.

Erwin, Allen, *The Southwest of John H. Slaughter.* Glendale: The Arthur H. Clark Company, 1965.

Davis, Elmer E., "Where the Ancient and Modern Meet — Tanque Verde Ranch," *The Great Southwest,* Vol. 7 (September, 1928).

Fitch, James Marston, *Architecture and the Aesthetics of Plenty.* New York: Columbia University Press, 1961.

Fontana, Bernard L., "Johnny Ward's Ranch" *The Kiva,* Vol. 28 (October-December, 1952).

Forbes, Robert Humphrey, *The Penningtons.* Lancaster: The New Era Printing Company, 1919.

Froebel, Julius, *Seven Years Travel in Central America, Northern Mexico, and the Far West of the United States.* London: Richard Bentley, 1859.

Gerald, Rex C., *Spanish Presidios of the Late Eighteenth Century.* Santa Fe: Museum of New Mexico Press, 1968.

Gordon, Clarence W., "Report on Cattle, Sheep and Swine, Supplementary to Livestock on Farms in 1880," *Tenth Census of the United States, 1880.* Washington: Government Printing Office. 1883.

Gowans, Alan, *Images of American Living.* Philadelphia: J. B. Lippincott Company, 1964.

Haskett, Bert, "Early History of the Cattle Industry in Arizona," *Arizona Historical Review,* Vol. 6 (October, 1935).

Heffner, Harry L., letter to Mary Boice Souders, Feb. 5, 1954, and recorded interview with Charles Pickerell, June 4, 1960, Special Collections, University of Arizona Library.

Hill, Gertrude, "Henry Clay Hooker: King of the Sierra Bonita," *Arizoniana,* Vol. 2 (Winter, 1961).

[Hislop, Herbert], *An Englishman's Arizona: The Ranching Letters of Herbert R. Hislop, 1876–1878.* Tucson: The Overland Press, 1965.

Hopkins, R. C., *Spanish Land Grants in America.* San Francisco: Privately Published, 1877.

Hooker, Forrestine Cooper, *The Long, Dim Trail.* New York: A. A. Knopf, 1920.

Hooker, Jessie P., "Four Generations of Hookers," *Arizona Cattlelog,* Vol. 5 (December, 1949).

Kniffen, Fred, "Folk Housing: Key to Diffusion," *Annals of Association of American Geographers,* Vol. 100 (December, 1965).

Kubler, George, *Mexican Architecture of the Sixteenth Century,* Vol. 1. New Haven: Yale University Press, 1948.

Lockwood, Frank C., "Pete Kitchen: Arizona Pioneer and Ranchman," *Arizona Historical Review,* Vol. 1 (April, 1928).

————. "Tucson: The Old Pueblo," *Arizona Historical Review,* Vol. 3 (April and July, 1930).

————. "One Thousand Acres on Potrero Creek," *Arizona Daily Star,* November 3, 1940.

Mackie, David C., editor, *Historic Architecture of Tucson.* City of Tucson, 1971.

Martin, Douglas D., *The Lamp in the Desert.* Tucson: The University of Arizona Press, 1960.

Mattison, Ray H., "Early Spanish and Mexican Settlements in Arizona," *New Mexico Historical Review,* Vol. 21 (October, 1946).

McClintock, James H., *Arizona,* Vol. 3. Chicago: S. J. Clarke Publishing Company, 1916.

Morrison, Hugh., *Early American Architecture from the First Colonial Settlements to the National Period.* New York: Oxford University Press, 1952.

Munk, Joseph A., *Arizona Sketches.* New York: The Grafton Press, 1905.

Myrick, David F., *Pioneer Arizona Railroads.* Golden: Colorado Railroad Museum, 1968.

Newcomb, Rexford, *Spanish Colonial Architecture in the United States.* New York: J. J. Augustin, 1937.

Olgyay, Victor, *Design With Climate.* Princeton: Princeton University Press, 1963.

Powell, H. M. T., *The Santa Fe Trail to California, 1849–1852,* edited by Douglas S. Watson. San Francisco: The Book Club of California, 1931.

Rapoport, Amos, *House Form and Culture.* Englewood Cliffs, N. J.: Prentice-Hall, 1969.

Report of the Governor of Arizona to the Secretary of the Interior, 1889, 1893, 1896. Washington: Government Printing Office, 1889, 1893, 1896.

Report of the Secretary of the Interior [1893], Vol. 3. Washington: Government Printing Office, 1893.

Reps, John A., *A History of City Planning in the United States.* Princeton: Princeton University Press, 1965.

Rice, David Talbot, *Islamic Art.* New York: Frederick A. Praeger, 1965.

Riggs, Jeanette Roll, *Our Eldorado.* Privately Printed, 1957.

Richardson, Rupert Norval, *The Greater Southwest*. Glendale: Arthur H. Clark Company, 1935.

Sanford, Don Alonzo, Record Book, Ms., Collection of Louise McKee Summers.

Sanford, Trent Elwood, *The Story of Architecture in Mexico*. New York: W. W. Norton & Company, 1947.

Schaus, Richard G., "Edward Bert Perrin," *Arizona Cattlelog*, Vol. 25 (August, 1968).

Sexton, R. W., *Spanish Influence on American Architecture and Decoration*. New York: Brentano, 1927.

Slaughter, Cora Viola, Memoirs, Ms., February 5, 1939, John Slaughter Collection, Arizona Historical Society, Tucson, Arizona.

Smith, Cornelius C., "Some Unpublished History of the Southwest: An Old Diary Found in Mexico," *Arizona Historical Review*, Vol. 6 (January, 1935).

Stanislawski, Dan, "Early Spanish Town Planning in the New World," *The Geographical Review*, Vol. 37 (January, 1947).

Steele, A. T., "The Lady Boss of Faraway Ranch," *The Saturday Evening Post*, Vol. 241 (March 15, 1958).

Underhill, Reuben L., *From Cowhides to Golden Fleece*. Palo Alto: Stanford University Press, 1939.

Wagoner, J. J., *History of the Cattle Industry in Southern Arizona, 1540–1940*. Tucson: University of Arizona Press, 1952.

———. "Overstocking of the Ranges in Southern Arizona during the 1870s and 1880s," *Arizoniana*, Vol. 2 (Spring, 1961).

Waterman, Thomas Tileston, *The Early Architecture of North Carolina*. Chapel Hill: University of North Carolina Press, 1947.

Wayland, Jane Abigail, "Experiment on the Santa Cruz: Colin Cameron's San Rafael Cattle Company, 1882–1893." Unpublished Master's thesis, University of Arizona, 1964.

Webb, Walter P., *The Great Plains*. Boston: Ginn and Company, 1931.

Willson, Roscoe G., *Pioneer and Well Known Cattlemen of Arizona*, Vol. 2. Phoenix: Valley National Bank, 1956.

Zinsmeister, Lee G., "The Old Sanford Ranch," *Westward Ho*, Vol. 1, (November-December, 1929).